WITHDRAWN

THE RELIGIOUS THOUGHT
OF
SAMUEL TAYLOR COLERIDGE

Orig. wood-engraving by GEORGE BUDAY, R.E.

THE RELIGIOUS THOUGHT OF SAMUEL TAYLOR COLERIDGE

David Pym

With a Foreword by
John Coulson

BARNES & NOBLE

BOOKS
10 East 53d St., New York 10022
(a division of Harper & Row Publishers, Inc.)

Copyright © 1978 Colin Smythe Ltd.

Published in the U.S.A. 1979 by Harper & Row Publishers, Inc.,
Barnes & Noble Import Division

Library of Congress Cataloging in Publication Data

Pym, David
The religious thought of Samuel Taylor Coleridge.
Includes bibliographical references and index.
1. Coleridge, Samuel Taylor, 1772-1834 – Religion
and ethics. 2. Christianity and literature.
I. Title
PR4487.R4P9   1978b   821'.7   78-14840

ISBN 0-06-495750-0

Printed in Great Britain

Contents

Foreword

A new book on Coleridge is always welcome. It is bound to reveal something about this remarkable man we did not know before, since what Dr Johnson said of Burke may be applied equally to Coleridge – his stream of mind was perpetual. This applies especially to his theology, and this book shows how various were the sources of that theological originality.

Coleridge lived in an age which had barely woken from its dogmatic slumbers, as witness the fate of his disciple, F. D. Maurice, when he tried to awaken the next generation from its dreams of eternal punishment. In such circumstances, the layman could assume a freedom of speculation (as he still may) denied to the cleric. Not that Coleridge would have been content to remain 'a clerically-minded Englishman'. He took the trouble to go to Europe, and was one of the first Englishmen to read Schleiermacher; but it is his ability to express what he found there in *our* ways of thinking which is one of the chief sources of his continuing value for us today.

But there are other and perhaps more profound reasons for his stature as a theologian. Dr Pym draws our attention to what is often mistaken for indolence, viz., an increasing *diffidence* in publishing his religious thoughts. This, Dr Pym argues, is evidence of a proper modesty, arising as it does from Coleridge's deepening sense of the reality of his faith. As his sufferings and misfortune increased, so he himself came to resemble his Mariner – 'alone on a wide wide sea'.

Religion was at the centre of his life; it had been so from the start; and no proper grasp of his literary achievement – as poet or critic – is possible when this fact is denied or set aside. In 1795, when he was still only twenty-three, and the French Revolution only some six years old, he had said: 'If we would have no Nero without, we must place a Caesar within us, and that Caesar must be religion'. During the summer which followed, he abandoned his utopian dreams of Pantisocracy, met Wordsworth for the first time, and married Sara Fricker – the Ancient Mariner was launched.

This book will help the reader to understand the terms and conditions which, in the end, made a landfall possible.

JOHN COULSON

1. A Great Man?

What constitutes that elusive quality termed 'greatness'? This is a question that men have continually asked, seeking for some simple formula, as the alchemist hungered for the philosopher's stone. Sometimes a person is so obviously great that both their contemporaries and those of future times have no need to delve into the matter. In their own special ways, William Shakespeare and Sir Isaac Newton have imprinted their work on the minds of countless readers, and without them the history of western culture would not be the same. Then we have those whose work has been in the political or military or practical sphere. They too have their claim to recognition.

Yet beware of the march of time. It is like a sea on which the reputations of men bob like corks. Sometimes it is seen that a man has been given too high a reputation, so in compensation he sinks for a while in total obscurity. There are also examples of the opposite process. Then we have the enigma, of which D. H. Lawrence is a prime example in recent times. Some have seen lasting importance in his work, while T. S. Eliot regarded him as a mere 'researcher into religious emotion'. It is easier for a man who has worked in several spheres of human activity to be classed as an enigma. The achievement of a Kant, a Newton, or a Napoleon stands out clearly, but a lifetime of diverse activity can too readily be classified as that of either a superman or a dilettante. Samuel Taylor Coleridge is a supreme example of this. A great poet, a student of the history of philosophy, the man who brought English theology out of the eighteenth-century into the Romantic era, and the teacher of the whole of the liberal Anglican school of Maurice, Sterling, Thirlwall and company, seems to be adequate claim for a place among England's greatest sons. However, there are many unattractive sides to his character. He was of an unstable character, he made a foolish marriage and was early addicted to opium, his publishers had to wait unreasonably long for the slightest sign of effort, and he was for ever exploiting

9

the charity of his friends and benefactors. Moreover, when we come to evaluate what he did put on paper, we have the unenviable task of wading through volumes of illegible jottings to find those priceless pearls among so much nonsense. So while the Wordsworths would do anything for him, perceiving his genius, even his sympathetic publisher Joseph Cottle was compelled to observe that 'of all men Mr Coleridge was the least qualified to display periodical industry'.[1] That caustic contemporary reviewer, William Hazlitt, concluded in 1825 that, with the exception of his early period of poetic activity, Coleridge's life had been wasted on sophistic *gossip*.[2]

However, this is far from being the whole story. At periodic intervals there have been men of stature who have seen that element of lasting significance in Coleridge. Coleridge was deeply Christian in his thinking; this was the last thing John Stuart Mill would have claimed. But he had the privilege as a very young man of joining that close circle of Milman and Maurice, Hare and Sterling, at the house of Dr Gillman, Coleridge's latter-day benefactor, and here they heard the great man just talk. The result was that Mill placed Coleridge on the same level as his father's great friend Jeremy Bentham.[3] In 1856 that most reticent of scholars, F. J. A. Hort, thought it worthwhile to contribute a brief but thoughtful study of Coleridge to *Cambridge Essays*. Contemporaries of this time, such as F. D. Maurice, James Martineau, Charles Kingsley, and Robertson of Brighton, also expressed their respect for Coleridge's religious teaching, but after this his influence declined, so that the later Victorians only knew him by the presence of his poems and the little devotional manual *Aids to Reflection* on their library shelves.

After the First World War Englishmen looked at Coleridge afresh. Alfred Cobban made a good study of Coleridge's political theory in *Edmund Burke and the Revolt against the Eighteenth-Century* (1929), but others tried to move too fast. Professor J. H. Muirhead attempted to see in Coleridge the complete basis of the idealism of Green, Caird, and company at the end of the century. After leaving such rich and diffuse teaching in abeyance for so long, we need much more careful preparation for it to unfold itself to us. Unfortunately over-eagerness has been the pattern, notably in American students of literature. Mill gives us the warning. He was wise enough to see that at least as far as his theology and metaphysics are concerned, Coleridge needs long and careful study and reflection. 'The time is yet far distant when, in the estimation of Coleridge, and his influence upon the intellect of our time, anything like unanimity can be looked for. As a poet, Coleridge has taken his place.' We have not moved far from here. So any study upon the theological and metaphysical achievement of Coleridge must at this stage in time concern itself with putting aside misconceptions and laying a few, it is to be hoped solid, foundation stones.

Now I am sure the reader will recognize that even with such recluses as Spinoza and Kant, it is not possible to explain their work properly without some account being taken of the circumstances of their lives. Work and life cannot exist in total isolation from each other, and this is especially true of such a turbulent existence as that of Coleridge. A good biography of Coleridge has been written by E. K. Chambers, but to save time a few salient biographical details should be sketched here.

Samuel Taylor Coleridge was born at Ottery St Mary in Devonshire in 1772, the son of the local vicar and schoolmaster. He was at school at Christ's Hospital, where he developed a love of poetry, notably that of the now forgotten William Lisle Bowles. His stay at Jesus College, Cambridge, began with early success, but an unwillingness to apply his talents in an ordered manner, especially to mathematics, and a marked tendency to debt led to his fleeing into the army, from which his elder brother secured his release. An ill-advised scheme to found a new 'Pantisocracy' in America meant he had to find money and a wife. He met the latter requirement by the long regretted step of hastily marrying Southey's sister-in-law, Sarah Fricker. After delivering some little-known but important theological lectures in Bristol in 1795 and failing at the same time to make a commercial success of his radical journal *The Watchman*, he thought of supplying his material needs as a Unitarian minister. Then an annuity by Josiah and Thomas Wedgwood prevented this. After collaborating with Wordsworth to produce the *Lyrical Ballads*, he went to Germany in 1799. Here he gained that knowledge of Kant, Spinoza, and Lessing that was to be of such significance in the development of his thought. Soon after he wrote the last of his great poems, and his life became dominated by a vicious circle of an increasing sense of failure in work and marriage, and a corresponding increase in his addiction to opium. In 1804 he went to Malta as a minor government official, and as we shall see, this had a profound influence on his religious thinking. He then set up as a public lecturer, his series on Shakespeare and other poets (1810-13) being the most successful, and he even had his tragedy *Remorse* produced at Drury Lane. In 1816 were published *Lay Sermons* and the following year *Biographia*

Literaria. Spending his closing years in the care of Dr James Gillman, a medical practitioner, he produced the popular *Aids to Reflection* (1825), and in 1830, four years before his death, *On the Constitution of Church and State.* It was during these final years that the bright young men from Cambridge and London, who were to be the leaders of the Broad Church Movement, came to hear hour upon hour of discourse and were content to forego the modern activity of discussion. Finally, after his death, there appeared the *Confessions of an Enquiring Spirit.*

So, after all, Coleridge's list of publications is not unimpressive. Yet they are really the tip of the iceberg. Because of the undisciplined nature of his habits, he could prepare little of his thought for the press, and therefore it is to his notebooks, to which he almost daily confided his thoughts, that we shall so often turn in order to get at the heart of what he has to offer us.

2. Who is God?

Think of the Romantic Movement in England and the name of Coleridge is never far away. Many of the principal figures – Wordsworth, Coleridge, Southey, Shelley – were young men searching for something during their formative years at the turn of the last century. They had discovered that nature is alive, an organic unity that breathes and moves, and they knew that man did not merely passively observe it, but used his faculties to mould and live in the process. Movement, light, warmth – this was their discovery, and their poetry was their expression of it all. No longer were they interested in the machine portrayed as the world by the deists and some of the British empiricist philosophers; thirsting after a God they could experience no more could they be content with their First Cause or Architect; perceiving life and power in their own minds no longer could they accept the current theory initially set forth by Locke, and developed by Hartley and Priestley, that we passively absorb and categorize like a modern computer those signals we receive through our senses. The others were on the whole content to allow such religion as they had to be dissolved in poetic feelings. But Coleridge was the great exception. He, of all the early English Romantics, was the only one to try seriously to put his feelings into an expression that was both Christian and metaphysical. His background and temperament demanded this, and demanded it long before he was thirty years old.

To begin at the beginning, Coleridge's quest for inward, warm, experiential religion began at school when he delved into Boehme's *Aurora*. By 1796 he had made a study of the Moravians, and devoured the writings of such as Swedenborg, Richard Baxter, and Giordano Bruno. Yet he soon perceived that a full religion demands the head as well as the heart of a man. So at first he turns to David Hartley to provide a philosophical framework for his consciousness of God.

13

From Hope and firmer Faith to perfect Love
Attracted and absorbed: and centred there
God only to behold, and know, and feel,
Till by exclusive consciousness of God
All self-annihilated it shall make
God its identity: God all in all!
We and our Father one! [1]

At the age of twenty-two in these *Religious Musings* we have the appearance of that one conviction that was to permeate nearly all his work; that belief that man can only obtain the state of perfect bliss in total communion with God. But to even attempt to give it a basis in philosophy was the hallmark of a great mind. That other great influence on Victorian theology, John Henry Newman, was nearly seventy before he produced a formal statement on the relation between faith and reason in postulating the 'illative sense', which is supposed to allow us to reach religious certainty by a process outside the knowledge provided by facts. [2]

Coleridge had made a start in this difficult task of relating a formal theory of knowledge to faith, but with the Romantic's consciousness of the value and richness of the human mind he could not for long accept any notion that left our faculties 'all self-annihilated'. So he turned his attention to another and greater philosopher, Bishop Berkeley, and fixed on his maxim taken from Acts 17.28, that God is him in whom 'we live, and move, and have our being'. [3] Here was a philosophical statement of the immanence of God into which Coleridge could dovetail the understanding of disclosure to the human mind he was gaining most notably from the Quaker George Fox with his concept of the 'inner light'. But the Romantic mind could not rest here. It has to respond to God's disclosure: it has to have a faculty whereby man can have a mystical vision of God, whereby he is not totally crushed by the revealing power of God, but keeps his own identity in his vision of and communion with his Creator. This is where Spinoza comes in.

We would be mistaken to suppose that Coleridge was the only one at the turn of the nineteenth century to discover Spinoza. Wordsworth, Shelley and Jacobi all found something in him; indeed 'Kant and Spinoza became the poles about which the thought of the . . . generation moved.' But we must concern ourselves with Coleridge, with his desire for a concept that stated the unity of man with God whilst at the same time preserving their separate personalities, and with the end of his quest in the formulation of the faculty of 'the primary imagination'. In September 1799 he could tell Southey that he was 'sunk in Spinoza', and by November of the same year his private notebook jottings tell us that Spinoza was satisfying the demand for unity. 'If I begin a poem of Spinoza, thus it should begin/I would make a pilgrimage to the burning sands of Arabia . . . to find the Man who could explain to me there can be *oneness*. . . .'[4] Of all the major seventeenth and eighteenth century philosophers only Spinoza escaped from the dualism of mind and matter; only he gave a metaphysical statement of God, man and nature which placed to the fore the immanence of God, the personality of man, and the organic quality of Creation; only he could postulate a real alternative to Descartes and say not *cogito, ergo sum,* but *homo cogitat.* This Coleridge realised, and by 1802 he had worked out, within of course the context of poetry, the character of *imagination* which gives to everything its own entity and men their autonomous personalities whilst all subsist in the immanence of God. Poetry for Coleridge has a sacramental quality, and the great poetic mind has the *imagination* to comprehend this.[5]

By this time the reader is thinking that the story is sketchy. But there are two things that we have to realize. At this time Coleridge's brain was riddled with opium which prevented him producing a long systematic account of his discovery, and secondly, he was facing the problem of incorporating Spinoza into his deeply Christian idea of God and avoiding the slightest taint of pantheism. For Coleridge God is not the *absconditus deus* of the deists or of Paley. As far as man goes, he is always the supereme subject as he continually creates and acts within the world. It was in the period of his lowest addiction to opium that he managed a formal statement of the 'primary imagination'. This is the faculty that reconciles the truth of the Christian understanding of a God both supreme and personal, and also immanent, with the fact of the independent human personality and intellect. We cannot avoid quoting this passage of the *Biographia Literaria* for it sets Coleridge's theological development in complete perspective.

> The imagination. . . . I consider either as primary, or secondary. The primary imagination I hold to be the living power and prime agent of all human perception, and as a repetition in the finite mind of the eternal act of creation in the infinite I AM.[6]

There is a passage in Spinoza's *Ethics* which almost seems to have been taken *en bloc* by Coleridge, and in this case he would seem to have little claim to greatness. But the imagination is only half the story, or rather less. Coleridge never departed from the basic Christian doctrine that God discloses himself to men in a personal way. The primary imagination is the philosophical statement of man's response; it is a metaphysical safeguard of the autonomy of the human intellect without sacrificing the Scriptural tenet of *imago dei*, the belief that the intellect of man is but a finite repetition of the infinite mind of God. It is the human response to God's disclosure.

An obvious question springs to the reader's mind. Why was Coleridge more advanced in formulating man's response to God in the world than God's revelation to man, which he always maintained came first? The answer has its biographical roots: revelation has never been the strong point of a Unitarian. But Unitarianism might have initially impeded the development of Coleridge's theology, yet it conferred an enormous blessing on it in the long term. The prevalent utilitarian rationalism of divines even of the Church of England, such as William Paley and Richard Watson, were so concerned with God as the great designer that they practically ignored his love set forth to men in Jesus of Nazareth. The Unitarians, through transferring some of the human characteristics of Jesus to their one God, were unique in England at the end of the eighteenth century in having any real concept of the personality of God. At Cambridge, Coleridge had come under the influence of that eminent member of the Unitarian movement, William Frend, with the result that in his 'Religious Musings' of the time we have a striking presentation of personality in God which he introduced later into theological orthodoxy.

> Lovely was the death
> Of Him whose Life was Love! Holy with power
> He on the thought-benighted Sceptic beamed
> Manifest Godhead, melting into day

Personality is pointless in isolation. If God is to have personality, so must man. The eighteenth century had always been eager to assign man a place and function similar to every other physical organism. The novel *Robinson Crusoe*, for example, takes great pride in the way that man succeeds as a 'natural mechanic' when circumstances demand. David Hartley spent great effort in explaining the entire working of the mind in terms of the functions of rods and other pieces of machinery. But life for Coleridge is more than a juxtaposition of particles, and man cannot be explained as an assembly of parts. So resounded the voice of a great Romantic. In utter contrast to most contemporary English thinking, he viewed man as an *organic* unity in which body, mind and spirit are fused into one; where life and mind lose their identities in mutual inter-penetration. In Coleridge's view, to be human means to be cogn-izant, moral and religious. In other words he demonstrated another characteristic break with the eighteenth century in the very fact of striving for an anthropology that we would call 'personal' in a truly modern sense.

As with all of Coleridge's metaphysical concepts, the seeds were sown in the first thirty years of his life, but we have to wait until after 1815 for their final development into a system of Christian philosophy, the rough draft of which appears in his later private notebooks. So it was with the development of the idea of person-ality. He read so much and it all had to be fermented, and filtered through his complex mind before it was ready for a place in any theological system. Surprisingly enough, although he detested Descartes' epistemology, he was prepared to draw on his discovery that consciousness is a vital element in being human. Before Descartes, the term 'subjective' referred not to one's personal feeling and understanding, but merely denoted things as they are in themselves, and objective described what belongs to them as presented to our consciousness. From him sprang the view that self-consciousness is the basis of personality, and although Cole-ridge rejected most of his thought in his early reading of him before 1804, twenty years later he took this element into his system. 'There can', his diary says, 'be no personality *without* Unity. . . . Now this without consciousness is animal Life – but . . . add Consciousness, and you have *Person*.'[7]

If Descartes aided Coleridge in clarifying his position, it was nothing to the contribution from the work of Kant, and we must remember that Coleridge was one of the very first Englishmen to study deeply the writings of the man who represents the philo-sophical watershed between the Enlightenment and the nineteenth century. More than any other contributing factor, he enabled Coleridge to bring English theology away from the determinism of rationalist thought into a modern appraisal of man and God, and indeed into one that is much closer to the doctrine of Scrip-ture. In distinguishing the practical from the pure reason, and setting the freedom of the will as a necessary postulate of the practical reason, Kant set the will in a sphere beyond any ration-alistic interpretation. Coleridge seized on this idea of the autono-mous will as the basis of personality, and used it as a weapon against the deistic tradition of Locke and Hartley, whom he used as a synonym for Priestley and Paley, in their desire to cast man down as a part with a predetermined function in the machine called Nature. Indeed, in *A Lay Sermon* he went so far as to say that the 'scientific' psychologists' refusal to recognize the special autonomy of the will was none other than a denial of the Christian doctrine of Atonement. It seems so obvious to us that the essence of personality is the consciousness of self and the freedom of the will that it is difficult to realize the effort Coleridge had to use to establish this. Without his work not only his own theology but that of Julius Hare, F. D. Maurice and Robertson of Brighton, to name but three, would have been much the poorer.

As usual, Coleridge not only borrowed; he developed, and in order to have a truly modern interpretation of God as a personal being, he extended to the Deity Kant's conclusions on the special character of man. Except in his little known work *Opus Postumum* which appeared in 1803, just before his death, Kant never wished to go as far as to ascribe personality to God. Kant, we have seen, stood on the brink of the nineteenth century, but theologically he never belonged to it. It is to his credit that he raised ethics above the criteria of a deistic scheme that subjected everything to mechanical laws, but in his great work on theology and moral philosophy, *The Critique of Practical Reason*, he committed the old rationalist heresy of a 'God in the gaps' in a new mode. The God of Kant isn't primary, he isn't self-evident in the believer's experience, but appears as a mere 'postulate' to render meaningful and render a reward to the man in the next life who is penalised for acting according to conscience.

This philosophical God is a long way from the God of the Bible, who is always taking the initiative and is always the supreme subject in his dealings with men. It is also a long way from the God of Boehme, Pascal, George Fox, and William Law, and it was from his own inward religious experience mirrored in these writers that he felt the need to give a metaphysical account of the personal God whom the Christian comes to know in a most intimate way. It seems likely that Coleridge learned the value of feeling early in his life at Christ's Hospital from his experience of poetry, especially that of William Lisle Bowles. But in his reading he soon turned to those writers who applied emotion to the question of knowing God. By 1803 he had learned that those with Pantheistic tendencies were going to provide little in the construction of a Christian philosophy, and from about that time he began to turn to George Fox, Richard Baxter,[8] and Pascal[9] in order to formulate the place of experience in theology. Especially was Fox vital to the development of his theology, with his teaching on the 'inner light'. In December 1802 he could write from the heart to a Unitarian friend John Prior Estlin: 'My creed is very simple – my confession of Faith very brief. I approve altogether & embrace entirely the *Religion* of the Quakers, but exceedingly dislike the sect. . . . By Quakerism I understand the opinions of George Fox. . . .'[10]

Thus we can see that Coleridge needed a personal God in the same way that he needed a personal view of man. A human personality can only be spiritually satisfied in a personal God. But how was Coleridge to have the metaphysical justification for adapting Kant's teaching on man to apply to God? Here as usual, he turned to the knowledge he had on hand; in this case that of Plato and those who learned from him. People have wondered why Coleridge came to study the Platonist tradition in such detail and overlook the fact that at Cambridge Plato was studied with more relish than at the Oxford of Coleridge's youth, and that he was more than a competent classical scholar until his wayward habits severed his link with formalised education. This study of Plato led on to a study of thinkers in the Platonist tradition that ebbed and flowed throughout the intellectual meanderings of Coleridge's life. In the autumn of 1796 he borrowed from the Bristol Library the 'Sermons' of Jeremy Taylor and Cudworth's *True Intellectual System of the Universe*. Wedgwood's annuity and the provision of a cottage in Nether Stowey accessible to the Bristol Library saved Coleridge from utter stagnation. In November of the same year he was so moved to study Platonism and its tradition that he asked Thelwall to buy a set of Neoplatonist writings.[11] By 1803 he had found the clue for his doctrine of God in the work of John Scotus Erigena, a ninth century Irish philosopher who attempted to reconcile the Neoplatonist notion of emanation with the Christian doctrine of creation. From his commonplace-books we can see that 1803 saw his mind fixing upon this aspect of Erigena's teaching.[12] This seems to have been a classic example of the development of the Coleridgean theology. He had relatively few original concepts of his own; the way of Coleridge was primarily to draw on a colossal knowledge of the history of culture and mould it into a part of a highly significant theological statement. In the development of English religious thinking he stood far above any other on the watershed between the absent divine mechanic of the eighteenth century with a closed, deterministic cosmology and the warmer, more personal and Biblical theology of the post-Romantic era. Coleridge was a young man in an England that looked for its apologetic to Paley and the systems of Priestley, Godwin,

Hartley and company which lay behind him. As early as 1796 he made the great step of dismissing 'the Godwinian System of Pride' in which man is 'an outcast of blind Nature ruled by a fatal Necessity'.[13] Soon after 1803 he set out upon another great venture and one that was to last his whole life; a metaphysical statement of the Biblical teaching of a free, personal, Trinitarian Godhead continuously in a saving relationship with personal man possessing free-will. And a great initial impetus to this was given in these years after 1803 by Coleridge finding in Erigena and other Platonists a justification for applying the 'principle of analogy' to Kant's doctrine of man centred upon the will. Of course the Bible also told Coleridge that a central inherent characteristic of God is his will. But it is typical of Coleridge to look for an equivalent metaphysical justification for every cardinal Biblical tenet. This he found initially in Erigena and a little later in Duns Scotus, who, in contrast to Aquinas, stressed the will and not the mind as the primary characteristic of God.[14] As we shall see in the following chapter this was central to Coleridge's teaching on the Atonement.

So, to summarise the story so far, Coleridge has his personal statement of what is a man. He has a personal God with mind and will who is continuously at work within the universe. But how is he to think of God as immanent and personal without dethroning him from the otherness and supremity which is cardinal to the teaching of the Bible? The obvious answer and the one given by the Fathers is the doctrine of the Trinity. But because of Coleridge's place in history on the brink between Rationalism and Romanticism it was far from being an obvious device for him to use. Since the first onslaught of the Reformation the cultural moods of the various eras were more and more having the final ruling in what theology could say, with the result that the traditional formulae were either being ignored or cramped in their meaning. The eighteenth century kept something of the otherness and majesty but lost God's immanence both in nature and in the soul of the believer: the nineteenth century romantics and liberals tended toward the opposite extreme; Schleiermacher mirrors this in placing his brief statement on the Trinity as little more than an appendage to his great dogmatic work *The Christian Faith*. Coleridge leant to neither extreme, and it was his admiration for Scripture, the Fathers, Luther and the Caroline divines that saved the future Broad Church movement from the extremities put forward by counterparts on the Continent.

Naturally this didn't come all at once. The lectures he gave at Bristol in 1795 show a young radical in politics and Unitarian in religion attacking vehemently the Church of England for confessing belief in the Trinity and the Atonement. He was on the brink of entering the Unitarian ministry and well would he have upheld their cause, attacking continually the Church of England as a haven for time servers. The twofold accusation of heresy and corruption shows us the uncertainty of a young man of twenty-three, and the end of what is apparently the fourth lecture particularly indicates this. 'When Christians had permitted themselves to receive as Gospel the idolatrous Doctrine of the Trinity, and the more pernicious dogma of Redemption, it is not wonderful that an Episcopal Church should be raised, fit superstructure for such foundations!' 1795 was indeed the year and really the only year when Coleridge was truly a man of the eighteenth century. It took a little while longer for him to finally decide to centre all his theology upon the doctrine of the Trinity. Here again his reading of others was crucial to his development. Spinoza again has a place, for the inadequacy of his pantheistic God drives Coleridge to seek for something better. He seems to have been an umbrella under which Coleridge sheltered around 1800 after fleeing from rationalism and Unitarianism. But he was only a philosophical umbrella. Coleridge in his heart must have been close to orthodoxy when he became infatuated with the writings of Berkeley and such as Law and Baxter before the turn of the century. Yet as we know metaphysics and revelation went hand in hand for Coleridge. If one went ahead in his thinking, the other had to be given time to catch up. Yet where was Coleridge to find the teaching of the Bible in a systematic and metaphysically-based form? Thirty and forty years later Newman was to solve his great religious dilemma by an analysis of the Fathers. But his quest was for historical authority and not metaphysical certainty. This explains why Coleridge was to differ from him in turning to those other great sources of Anglican inspiration, the Reformers and the Caroline divines. It was his reading of Hooker that led him to exclaim 'that the Trinity is the only Form, in which an Idea of God is Possible – unless indeed it be a Spinozistic or World-God.'[15] By this time Coleridge had already attributed a will to God, which safely prevents any looking back to pantheism,[16] and so he must press on to the answer the Carolines can provide him with.

Coleridge was feeling his way. After 1795 his whole mood toward theology altered. No longer do we have the sweeping public statements which thundered from the lecture-hall platform at Bristol. In his lifetime and particularly during his middle years little of his theological achievement found its way into print. He could lecture on Shakespeare and men of letters, he could publish tracts on the periphery of theology dealing with Christianity and the state, but apart from *Aids to Reflection* the deep things of the soul were confided to his private notebooks, to his personal letters, and to friends and disciples. It has been the custom to attribute Coleridge's inability to get books into print to his drug addiction, the circumstances of his marriage and other aspects of his personal life. But with regard to theology this is only part of the story. It seems certain that his refusal to rush into public statements stemmed more from a sense of unworthiness than from the actual physical incapacity induced by laudanum. So it is not surprising that it was in a personal conversation during a social evening at Captain Burney's in August 1812 that Coleridge confided to his friend Crabb Robinson 'many remarks on the doctrine of the Trinity from which I could gather only that he was very desirous to be orthodox, to indulge in all the subtleties and refinements of metaphysics and yet conform to the popular religion.'[17] Credal orthodoxy, a serious metaphysic and a religion of inward warmth – these were the demands Coleridge set himself, and for an Englishman what a demand! In the persons of Schleiermacher, Rudolf Otto, Rudolf Bultmann and a galaxy of others the German tradition has often attempted this. Sometimes fearing that philosophy will ultimately impoverish the Christian content of any system, Englishmen have generally been content to use philosophy as an aid to formulating separate doctrinal statements or else, as in the case of Paley, earlier in the eighteenth century Butler, and later in the nineteenth J. B. Mozley, been satisfied to use philosophy for particular apologetic purposes, in their case as heirs of the deistic obsession with miracles. Berkeley, Newman, and in the present century William Temple, went beyond this, but only Coleridge of English theologians can justify the description of systematic. This seems rash praise indeed and one that would make him truly a great man if we could establish it. His published works are modest although significant for their own time, but, as we shall see, it is his unpublished notebooks written in the last twenty years of his life that show an understanding of the demands of theology and an attempt to master them that only Newman of the English nineteenth century can begin to match.

If the reader has had experience of preaching or writing he will know how easy it is to waver from the point of the Christian teacher of stating plainly things concerning God and man. In a man dealing with the entire European cultural tradition as the arena in which to express essential doctrine, the temptation was

22

all the more present. It would have been easier to write a book on the history of philosophy and it is all the more credit to Coleridge's much maligned staying-power that he never wavered from his certainty that the Trinity is 'the grand article of faith, and the foundation of the whole christian system'.[18] This is consistent with the character of a man who, perhaps the reader is surprised to learn, always had the Bible and Luther's *Table-Talk* at his bedside. This continual return to the basic doctrines of Christianity gave Coleridge the inspiration to keep working at his attempt to give a contemporary interpretation to the doctrine of the Trinity. From the Apologists of second century Rome until the writings of Barth, Bultmann and their followers in the present age, this has been the difficult function of many theologians. How well they succeeded can only be judged on two counts. First, there is the effect it had on the course of theology at the time, and, in the case of Coleridge, the acutely critical minds of Julius Hare and F. D. Maurice accepted his work with scarcely any fuss. Secondly, looking back over a century and a half, how great does it appear when measured against the perspective of theological attainment of the day?

This last point bears considerable attention which we can give before going into details of the great metaphysical interpretation of the doctrine of the Trinity which Coleridge sketched in the last twenty years of his life. We shall content ourselves with two observations. The first of these is Coleridge's remarkable independence of thought coupled with a vast knowledge of history both Christian and secular. This gave him the confidence to ignore the English eighteenth century as a mere shadow of the true Christian tradition and to build a theology on the doctrine of Luther and the Carolines, the metaphysic of Plato, Kant's analysis of man, and the sense of the inward drawn from such as Law and Baxter together with his own awareness as a Romantic. A cursory glance at Dorothy Wordsworth's *Journals* shows that he spent weeks on end meditating not only on nature but on things of the inward soul. Indeed as time went on, reflections on nature gave way more and more to those on the inward man. This is the clue to our second remark. Coleridge was really concerned to give a statement of the activity of God within individual men. This gave it a lasting value in setting it outside any possible conflict of revelation with scientific advance that plagued so much of the last century. Godwin's *Political Justice* and Paley's *Natural Theology*, both published at the turn of the last century, set forth a harmonious image of nature consistent with arguing for revelation from miracle. This was the classical English apologetic at the time, and led to the publication of the *Bridgewater Treatises*, which set forth the goodness and wisdom of God in creation. But even when Coleridge was a young man there were rumblings to disturb all these assumptions. Erasmus Darwin's *Zoonomia* (1794-6) put forward a theory of Evolution based on Hartley's psychology, and in 1798 Thomas Malthus published his gloomy forecast on population and food supply in his *Essay on the Principle of Population*. God's benevolence in nature, the corner-stone of English apologetic, was even then being challenged. In his theological lectures of 1795 Coleridge adhered to the coventional view in saying that 'what to the eye of Thomas Paine appears to be a chaos of unintelligibles, Sir Isaac Newton and John Locke and David Hartley discover to be miraculous order and Wisdom more than human.' But Coleridge was abreast of scientific advance. He knew Hutton's *Theory of the Earth* (1795), and early in 1796 actually met Erasmus Darwin in Nottingham while attempting to find a market for his ill-fated journal *The Watchman*. Here he was not impressed with Darwin's bigoted and partial reasoning. 'He boasted', wrote Coleridge to a friend, 'that he had never read one book in defence of such *stuff*, but he had read all the works of infidels! Would you think him an honest man?'[19] But Coleridge seems to be saying that argument about such matters is useless. His letter gives a sense of exasperation. He never again attempts to meet rationalist agnostics and atheists with miracles and prophecy, the weapons of Christian rationalism. He leaves nature in order to concentrate on the soul of man. He was always a Romantic with a love of feeling and warmth, but this becomes more and more transferred from the natural world to the spiritual and metaphysical. As an aside, I might add that I believe this is one reason for the decline in Coleridge's poetic activity after 1800. It is almost impossible to produce a saleable poem on the inward life of a man.

In his exposition of the Trinity, it is fair to say that Coleridge never saw himself as more than a part of the most orthodox Anglican tradition and merely developing the teaching of Daniel Waterland, that distinguished Archdeacon of Middlesex and holder of a dozen other offices, who, in the first third of the eighteenth century, had stemmed the flood of Unitarian and Arian tendencies within the established church. As one trying to cast off all vestiges of a Unitarian past, Coleridge would naturally have turned to his writings and came to value them very much. However, he did lament the fact that Waterland never attempted to ground his teaching in any formal metaphysic. 'Everywhere in this invaluable

Writer I have to regret the absence of a distinct *Idea* of the I Am, as the *proper* Attribute of the FATHER: and hence, the ignorance of the proper Jehovaism of the Son.'[20] In a moment we shall glance at this difficult topic of the place of God in Coleridge's logic and metaphysics, but it is interesting that considerations of epistemology added to his conviction of the significance of the Trinity. In part the Romantic revolt against the eighteenth century was against the dualistic outlook induced by the tradition of Descartes which set up an unbridgeable chasm between God and man, mind and matter, subject and object. And it was in Richard Baxter that Coleridge saw the first glimmer of a dissatisfaction with this position:

> We ought not to overlook, that the substitution of Trichotomy for the old & still general plan of Dichotomy in the Method and Disposition of Logic, which forms so prominent and substantial an excellence in Kant's Critique of the Pure Reason, of the Judgement, &c. belongs originally to Richard Baxter.[21]

Although Coleridge complained that 'Baxter often expresses himself so as to excite a suspicion that he was inclined to Sabellianism',[22] he seems to have given Coleridge the spark to work out the relation between logic and the Trinity. As early as 1806, practically simultaneous with, yet independent of the famous thesis, antithesis and synthesis of Hegel, Coleridge was exploring the possibility of seeing the Holy Spirit as the synthesis of the function of the other Persons of the Godhead.[23] By 1810 he had firmly made up his mind that when God reveals himself Trinitarianly, he is revealing himself according to 'the principle of trichotomy', as he described his logic. 'God and Truth – the Actuality of logic the very *Logos*',[24] wrote Coleridge in an otherwise obscure note.

After this Coleridge attempted to show how the Trinity has its counterpart in a true metaphysic. Partly because his system was left in a rough draft in his private notebooks, partly because of the difficulty of the task, and partly because he confused the language of Scripture and the Fathers with that of Kant and Plato, it is not always easy to see his position. But in brief I understand it to be this. When Coleridge makes God 'the Supreme Reason', 'the Idea Idearum', he is raising metaphysics to its highest sphere, the theological.[25] In any Christian metaphysic, the metaphysical statement of God must not become disconnected or discontinuous with the remainder or otherwise there is no longer a system. God can be at the apex of the system, but he can never be taken out of it. And this is precisely the point at which Coleridge shows us that he never really escaped from the outlook and assumption of the eighteenth century. He might stress the autonomy of God, and replace Locke and Toland's divine mechanic with this Christianised version of Kant's essentially ethical God. He might raise man above nature and reassert his personality and individuality. He might give a more Scriptural interpretation of faith and inward religion. Yet he is obsessed with the notion that the only really valid theology sets forth God, man and nature in a logically flawless and theologically exhaustive edifice. As we have said before, his attempt to be systematic was praiseworthy, but if only he could have been systematic as a Romantic, content to leave much unsaid to speak to the heart of man for itself, and not tried to explain every possible detail as if Priestley, Hume, Kant, Spinoza and Tom Paine were all looking over his shoulder at once, then we would not find that clarity had been sacrificed for the roundness of the system. And clarity is certainly lacking in some of Coleridge's statements on the character of God. It was certainly a step forward to use logic to expound the Trinity, but to push it to provide an exhaustive statement has led to confusion. It appears that Coleridge suffered from the same disease as his friend and contemporary Wordsworth. Wordsworth expressed it in his political notions and Coleridge in his theology; but from the age of about thirty-five their Romanticism was largely drawn from the fat they had stored in their love of life and the living and the individual expressed in their poetry and intellectual adventures before this time. From then on a desire to be ordered almost led to the extinguishing of the precious Romantic spark, and in the case of Coleridge we must be thankful that he incorporated into his system those concepts that had their roots in his thinking before 1805.

I shall now attempt to state in a short compass Coleridge's logic and doctrine of God. To avoid it, although to some dull and technical, is to avoid the heart of his whole theology, and so I trust the reader will bear with me for a page or two. Yet I hope that he who chooses to pass over it will be able to pick up our account a little later. Now the *Idea* is basic to Coleridge's system. It is not as we would imagine a concept, but is what is known as 'constitutive in itself'. Once again Coleridge follows Plato as opposed to Aristotle. In the highest level of all, that pertaining to God or theological, the Ideas of God are for Coleridge his characteristics. But where Coleridge really leads his reader into confusion is in assuming that because God revealed himself in history as Father, Son and Spirit, this doctrine can explain all about God before he even entered into the process of creation. This is a serious weakness of Coleridge's system and one that is closely linked with his other great failure in misunderstanding the nature of history. We get two Trinities almost. There is the one that is not known to us except through the mode of speculation. Here for Coleridge we are not only faced with comprehending the notion of the Will of God, but rather is it embedded in what is termed the Idea of the will. And this he decided is the supreme mystery.

> . . . the first Idea, i.e. the Idea of *Will* as the Absolute – essentially causative of all Reality, therefore of its own Reality . . . the Abysmal Mystery! . . . Each distinctive Idea in the Absolute Idea is a form of the Absolute Will. . . . For the Godhead alone in the three-fold Absolute, the Ipseity, and the Community, the Will, the Word and the Spirit, are in themselves Actus purissimus; sine ulla potentialitate – the Distinctities only as one with the Absolute, which they *will* to be –'[26]

What nonsense! To see revelation merely as a drawing back of the curtain hiding God's presence, to see rowed up all the contents of the revelation in history is not conducive to clarity or good sense. The idle dreamer at Christ's Hospital lived on in Coleridge's brain. We can on the one hand admire Coleridge for trying to form a Christian metaphysic, but we must point out his error. The Trinitarian Godhead as revealed in the Biblical revelation is the grand article of faith. As we shall see, Coleridge performed a great service in analysing this. But to speculate in the transcendent realm to such a degree can only lead to confusion. The over-ambitious side of Coleridge's mind, the weakness in indulging in idle speculation is most apparent in his theory that it is God as Word who is Idea Idearum because 'the whole Host of Ideas subsist in the Word, as the only begotten absolute Idea of the Father'.[27] Philosophy served Coleridge well. But he too readily allowed it to become his master, and drag some sublime thinking into the mire of nonsense. We too gain nothing by following this path and must pass on to places where his thought can enrich our thought and his faith instruct our faith.

3. Christus pro me, Deus pro nobis

Coleridge had his failure in trying to press a metaphysic too far in explaining the character of God. Yet nevertheless he had tried to produce a theology that spoke to both the head and the heart of man. The depth of knowledge brought together to attempt this is a mark of greatness and this greatness is never more manifest than in Coleridge's understanding of the effect of God on the individual soul of the believer. Time and again we hear the conviction of Luther's maxim that heads this chapter lying behind so many of Coleridge's utterances. In a note of 1827 he testifies to the importance that the great German reformer had for him. 'There have been moments', he writes, 'when the Spirit of Luther has pointed to a Trumpet. Truth, *the* Truth! the *Whole* Truth! So only can a People be made *free*.'[1] This is an influence that grew throughout Coleridge's life as he came to think with ever increasing intensity on the extremely personal subjects as a man's need for redemption, his conscience, his inward religion and faith, and above all on Christ and the sanctifying Spirit. Theology for Coleridge is an attempt to describe this in a systematic way.

In general theology can concern itself with any of three approaches. These are in evaluating the relation between God and the natural world, analysing the historical revelation described in the Bible, and examining the character of religion within man. It is fairly easy to understand why Coleridge had little confidence in any theological enquiry which set too much store by an historical approach. At this time in England there was little interest in history and especially in trying to ascertain what history really is. The assumptions of deism that the universe is a perfectly designed but static balance of forces still persisted in England until well into the nineteenth century. Therefore little need was perceived to study any historical development and nearly all Englishmen were content with Paley's apologetic which based the claim for revelation on miracle and prophecy. As he came to read the assault on the assumptions of the Enlightenment put forth by Kant and Hume, Coleridge saw Paley's argument for God and revelation were no longer valid. On the other hand we shall see in a later chapter that he had great difficulty in coming to terms with the Biblical witness to the acts of God in history. But for the present we shall concern ourselves with looking at the reasons for Coleridge's concern for the inward life of man.

It has been said that a study of Coleridge's thinking can be made with scarce reference to his experience of life. Of all men this cannot be defended in Coleridge! His life over the crucial years from 1795 to 1805 saw a change where a self-confident young man of twenty-three ready to go to America with a hastily married sister-in-law of Southey's in pursuit of an unobtainable political ideal, prepared to denounce the Established institutions of the land in a public lecture at Bristol, turned into a half withdrawn wreck becoming increasingly addicted to opium and having failed to make either a satisfactory career or marriage. In 1795 we see an optimism engendered by outward things. In his poetry for example the early years find his inspiration being drawn from the autumnal moon, the rose and his native River Otter in Devonshire. In 1798 his poem *The Nightingale*, evolved at the apex of his infatuation with Berkeley, shows that he had a moment when he could believe in a Platonism where Nature is permeated with a reflected divinity. He extols the nightingale

> .... so his fame
> Should share in Nature's immortality,
> A venerable thing! and so his song
> Should make all Nature lovelier, and itself
> Beloved like Nature! [2]

Confidence in outward things ruled Coleridge's heart in the mid 1790's. His mind was never again so ready to accept things without examination. Although he read so much and so widely as a young man he was quite prepared to hold conflicting outlooks in his mind at the same time. Whilst he held a Romantic view of Nature as a living and breathing organic unity, he was at the same time prepared to accept a view of history and man and ethics that was entirely rationalist and mainly from a Unitarian source.[3] One foot of Coleridge had already moved into the nineteenth century, whilst the other still dragged in the mire of a bankrupt Enlightenment.

In the years following 1789 the eyes of Europe were firmly fixed upon France. Many trembled at the thought of this pattern of revolt happening elsewhere. But among the Unitarians, who hated the subservience of religion to a temporal power and saw little good in the Church of England, there were a substantial part of those radical Englishmen who reckoned the French Revolution to be the first sign of a new age of freedom and justice.[4] Coleridge viewed these events in Paris through the same eyes and for this one brief phase in his life saw evil in terms of outward events and physical oppression and looked for God's provision of a political and historical solution. 'Religious Musings', a poem Coleridge began in 1794, sees the Paris turmoils as the final death throes of the old order, where religion was wed to wealth, and as the birth pangs heralding a new age in which faith and piety would be set free from any church that prostrates itself to the world. 'This passage', writes Coleridge in a footnote explaining the poem

> alludes to the French Revolution: and the subsequent paragraph to the downfall of Religious Establishments. I am convinced that the Babylon of the Apocalypse does not apply to Rome exclusively; but to the union of Religion with Power and Wealth, wherever this is found.[5]

It is true that the poem explains the sufferings of the French people in accordance with a Christian understanding of the final chapter of the Book of Job. The problem of evil can only be resolved in the light of the vision of God and final activity of Christ. But only in these early poems and the lectures given at Bristol in 1795 was he to attempt to see this activity in the occurrences of history. Henceforth all theodicy was to be perceived in terms of the individual soul.

However, no account of Coleridge can be complete without looking at these little known lectures for in the realm of theology they represent the high-point of Coleridge's rationalist phase. What with the Deistic conception of God, the rationalist logic-chopping, and the almost naive optimism, the Unitarian influence on him is never more apparent. For instance, he argues that to speak of an indifferent Deity is meaningless, for he must have created to some end. With the Enlightenment's characteristic of applying rationalist argument to God himself, Coleridge says that a malignant Deity is contrary to experience; and if he was ever a mixture of good and evil, one must overcome the other.

Developing the theme of 'Religious Musings', Coleridge has an even greater confidence in what we might call a 'teleological' solution to the problem of suffering: 'I have been able to discover nothing of which the end is not good.' Electing to use the word 'pain' as a contrast to evil which is moral in origin, he cites an example in an effort to verify this optimistic view of the ultimate benefit of suffering. Teeth, says Coleridge, give pain when we neglect them, but this is far outweighed by the benefit they confer in enabling us to eat. But this whole attitude is characteristic of a young man of twenty-three whose only suffering had been the result of his desultory approach to studies at Cambridge, a fool-hardy disregard for his debts, and finally joining the army as a cowardly way to avoid the consequences of folly. Even from these self-induced miseries his eldest brother, who had succeeded their father as vicar and schoolmaster of Ottery St Mary, readily relieved him with a little influence and a little more money. So it is little wonder that only months after these happenings Coleridge presented his audience with an explanation of evil and pain that was thoughtless and sprang not from the heart and experience. He was so involved with the Enlightenment's shallow but beauti-fully symmetrical view of nature where every part rests in a bene-volent and harmonious relationship with the rest, that he attributes all pain to man's wrongdoing, either by commission or omission. 'So shall we find that all through Nature that Pain is intended as a stimulus to Man in order that he may remove Moral Evil.' The shallowness of his explanation of pain is nowhere more explicit than in the statement that it 'is somehow or other the effect of Moral Evil'. This equation of sin and suffering fails to take account of the occasions when we see people in pain from disease or acci-dent who have committed no moral act worthy of such suffering or else do not know of the connection between their suffering and past actions; in which case the pain is meaningless. We can easily add that in many cases the destructive power of the suffering is so incapacitating that the person is rendered unable to make any move to rectify his past.

So, we must conclude, the Coleridge of 1795 was still very much entrenched in the eighteenth century's rationalist interpretation of suffering and its whole tradition of ethics. As with its view of Nature, facts and experience were sacrificed to belief in a sym-metrically balanced idea of 'rewards and punishment', and moral behaviour was practically identified with prudence. Yet the theo-logical lectures show a glimmer of hope. In comparison with the sentiments of 'Religious Musings', first set to paper the previous year, there is a definite cooling in attitude to the French Revolu-tion, and he differed significantly from his slightly older and very influential French contemporary Claude Saint-Simon, who gave it the classical positivist and socialist interpretation. Saint-Simon reckoned that 'progress', viewed in a naturalistic and deterministic way, is an inherent characteristic of human history whereas, even at this early stage, Coleridge has little confidence in the ability of man alone to reach a satisfying solution of his problems. Even at the height of his radicalism he still retained a God-centred outlook which was the seed of all his later thought. When he delivered these theological lectures he was convinced that ultimately a supernatural intervention by God is imperative, and this he saw as the purpose of the Messiah's mission. Passing over the question of the divinity of Christ in typical Unitarian manner, Coleridge told the audience at his lectures that the Messiah was sent in order that through faith man might come to a knowledge of God and thereby find his true personality and place in a properly integrated society to the total elimination of chaos and suffering.

After these lectures never again was Coleridge to set forward a 'teleological' or 'eschatological' solution to the problem of pain. When he realized that the French Revolution did nothing to explain the suffering it brought, when he found that it was not the birth pangs of an age of bliss but of a new era of tyranny, then he ceased trying to find a theodicy, a scheme of total justice, in the panorama of history. After he had lived a few more years he knew from his own experience that it is not history but individual man who suffers. And it is the individual person who needs to know why he suffers and how he sins and how he can be saved from both.

We shall pursue this later. But for the moment we shall pause to notice the historical significance of Coleridge's early exploration into the problem of evil. A 'theodicy' is a systematic attempt to explain the sufferings of man and the evil he propagates in terms of his sin and the atoning activity of God. In his very important book, *Evil and the God of Love*, Professor John Hick draws out the fact that there have been two traditions of theodicy within Christian theology, those after the respective approaches of Augustine and Irenaeus. The Augustinian tradition presents a unity in taking a much graver view of the Fall than the theologians of the Irenaean outlook. 'The fall ceases to be thought of – as generally by the Greek-speaking theologians – as a *deprivatio*, the loss of something good, and is seen as a *depravatio*, a wicked corruption.'[6] In contrast to Augustine, Irenaeus was not of the opinion that the time before the Fall shows man in absolute perfection, and he believed that the purpose of Christ's coming was to achieve more than merely the restoration of man to some primeval state. Both believed that the first man was able to enjoy a relationship with God, but Irenaeus was convinced he was incapable of using God's gifts to the full. According to Irenaeus, the sin of Adam and Eve should not be seen 'as a damnable revolt, but rather as calling forth God's compassion on account of his weakness and vulnerability.'[7] Through the work of the Son of God and his own response through faith, man is enabled to obtain a higher state and a closer relationship with God than the one originally imparted in Creation.

Although the approach of Irenaeus lived on in the Greek Fathers, the prestige of Augustine soon obliterated it from the mainstream of Christian thinking, and Hick believes that *The Christian Faith* of Schleiermacher, which appeared in 1821, heralded its return.[8] This makes Coleridge's theodicy put forward in 'Religious Musings' and the theological lectures at least a historical curiosity. In the poem he treats it as erroneous to attempt to return to the primeval mode of life, and he goes on to explain this view in the first of the lectures. Moral evil was implanted by God in order that man might gain a perfection beyond that of primeval innocence. 'Innocence implies the absence of Vice from the absence of Temptation. Virtue the absence of Vice from the knowledge of its consequences.' In short, Coleridge was striving to show that moral evil has a purpose and decided that it is a necessary part in the divine plan for man's achievement of perfection in which he has the pleasure of experiencing improvement, even though this ultimate state cannot be reached without the intervention of the Messiah.

As a passing point we ought to notice the decidedly modern ring in Coleridge's belief that moral evil leads to the destruction of man's personality and the disintegration of his relationship with God and his fellow men. But the vital question to ask and the important discovery to make is why Coleridge first of all postulated a highly original theodicy, and then decided to leave it entirely?

The answer to this is twofold. The first concerns Coleridge's attitude to the character of history itself. We shall look at this in more detail later; but for our present purposes it is sufficient to say that as Coleridge in 1795 thought very much as a man of the eighteenth century it is not surprising to learn that his understanding of history belonged very much to the same era. The world was seen as a closed and self-contained machine running according to the laws of Newtonian physics. There was no notion of evolutionary development. One event was much the same as another. A static balance was the key-concept in explaining the world, and this idea spilled over into the understanding of history and ethics. So we find in Coleridge's early thinking the classical eighteenth century notion of 'rewards and punishments', where every evil act must ultimately be punished and every good deed rewarded, so that justice may hold all in harmony.

However, as in much of Coleridge's outlook, the years between 1795 and 1805 provide a watershed in his outlook, and his stay in Germany during 1798-9 is of special importance. On the short term analysis his excellent translation of Schiller's *Wallenstein* was the only significant result of the travelling, but crucial was the meeting with the thought of Lessing, with his separation of the incidental truths of history from the necessary truths of reason. Never again was Coleridge to have the trust in any interpretation of history that he had in 1795, and never again was he to attempt to give a theodicy primarily within a historical context.

The second and more important reason for Coleridge turning away from history to the inward life of a man as the prime area of importance lies in the rather tragic passage which his own life followed. In 1795 there was a flamboyant young man who was prepared to dazzle the audiences of his lectures with all manner of outstanding dress. But by 1805 the picture was very different. In 1796 *The Watchman* failed and this heralded a lifetime of inability to meet obligations to publishers or to judge the likely outcome of any venture with all the financial uncertainty that such disabilities bring. Bound up with this and to add to his personal unhappiness, Coleridge soon found that he was temperamentally unsuited to his wife Sara, although he was devoted to his children and the death of his infant son Berkeley grieved him greatly. The year 1798 set his course towards decay. Being ill the previous summer, he had gone to live in an isolated farmhouse between Lynton and Porlock in North Devon. It seems that it was here that he first became acquainted with the effects of laudanum. At first it had the effect of relieving pain, but by the following May it had led to the composition of the visionary poem *Kubla Khan*. So began a slavery to opium that worsened any illness he might suffer and lasted with only the briefest intermissions throughout the remainder of his life. After his stay in Germany Coleridge settled with his family at Greta Hall, Keswick. But this marked the beginning of the final estrangement from his wife, and he spent more and more time with the Wordsworths at Grasmere, frequently staying for days at a time. Dorothy Wordsworth's Grasmere Journal sheds a great deal of light on Coleridge's life at this time. Only a man in a very strange mental state would leave one of his much-loved children in a state of grave illness and ride through inclement Lakeland weather to discuss a poem.

Coleridge came in while we were at dinner, very wet – we talked till 12 o'clock. He had sat up all the night before, writing Essays for the newspaper. His youngest child had been very ill in convulsion fits. Exceedingly delighted with the second part of *Christabel*.[9]

The final indication of a very unsatisfactory home life and peculiar state of mind began when Coleridge invited Southey and his homeless family to share Greta Hall. It was natural to invite in this way the husband of one's wife's sister and a man who shared many of his adventures with poetry, Pantisocracy and Unitarianism in the halcyon days when they first left university. But it was, to say the least, irresponsible to see this as an excuse to leave the unreliable agent of Southey's pen to provide for the support of both their families. In the subsequent years Southey may have produced two masterpieces in his *Life of Nelson* and *History of Brazil*, yet this does not exempt Coleridge from his shortcomings. But this was the very strange feature about Coleridge's thinking at this time and probably enhanced by imprudent use of laudanum. It appears that he carried Lessing's division between outward events and inward truths to its absurd extremity and played this out in his own life. At the same time as neglecting his obvious responsibilities he could spend a large amount of time reading such spiritual writers as Jeremy Taylor and George Fox and be able to write to John Thelwall: 'God bless the old Schoolmen! they have been my best comforts & most instructive Companions for the last 2 years.'[10] Oblivion to outward happenings went hand in hand with a retreat into his own mind, where he carried out a minute analysis of the state and needs of the human soul. Here in the inward self is the real character of humanity; this is the source of evil and weakness; to this place must come redemption and forgiveness. From 1803 onwards history definitely becomes secondary in Coleridge's thinking. Redemption is what happens in the inner man and it is the purpose of theology to analyse and describe it.

So we have discovered a strange feature of Coleridge's character. Outward misfortune over ten years caused him to turn inwards upon himself to such a degree that events around him became merely a background of echoes, a shadow of the drama happening within his soul. Only this kind of mental constitution could account for a man who stuffed page after page on the question of evil and redemption into dozens of personal notebooks, yet was so little concerned with the material well-being of his family. This is consistent with a theology where inward spiritual life is of overwhelming importance and the historical event of the Incarnation is almost superfluous. The development of this trait in Coleridge over the years following his return from Germany goes a long way towards solving the debate as to whether the external happenings in Coleridge's life had more than a superficial effect on the development of his thought. For far too long it has been the fashion to approach the study of Coleridge by taking a single poem or other feature of his work and by considering all the probable and improbable intellectual and cultural influences upon it as if the flesh and blood existence of Coleridge had negligible effect on what issued from his pen. Indeed Mr Humphrey House was fully justified in beginning his Clark Lectures of 1951-2 with the complaint that 'it is now a familiar line of approach to say that the outward events of Coleridge's life are of quite secondary importance, and that his history is the history of a mind.'[11] On the other hand there were only a few outward experiences, one of which we shall examine in a short while, which had a really significant effect on Coleridge's thought, and Mr House's view that 'once his illness and emotional frustration had established themselves as the norm of his daily life, *they* tended to govern the current stream of association'[12] overstates the opposite case. There is no point in examining a few passages obviously written under the influence of laudanum. Even when Coleridge was in a more normal state he had little notion of responsibility, and the life within the confines of his mind always interested him far more than that beyond it. Reality was within, and external things, be they his own experiences or those recorded in books or those of the contemporary religious or political situation, were the various foods upon which the mind fed. Putting this another way, external things were not there to be served by Coleridge's brain; rather they were lighthouses to guide it upon its all-important path.

This reorientation of outlook was sufficient in itself for one mind to contend with, and therefore it is hardly surprising that Coleridge kept silence upon the problem of evil until 1803. But suddenly he breaks his silence and reveals the line upon which his mind had been running: 'To return to the Question of Evil – woe to the man to whom it is an uninteresting question . . . the Question must be new, *new spicy hot* Gingerbread.'[13] Another note written at the same time tells us that Spinoza[14] has once more made his presence felt in Coleridge's mind as he played with the idea that pleasure and pain should not be held too far apart as they are both expressions of our finitude in comparison with the character of God. However he decided that pantheism is a denial of the omniscience of God, and, being a Christian interpreter of Kant, he concluded that God has given man 'a Duty to choose Good rather than evil'. Yet these jottings represent no fresh solution to the problem of suffering. Through his personal experience and his reading he is more aware of the various issues bound up with the problem, but as yet he can only say in basic prose what his meditations on France in 'Religious Musings' echoed in poetic terms. The final vision of God will make as nothing the difference between what we term good and evil: 'yet even now . . . our Cold & Darkness are so called only in comparison with the Heat and Light of the Coming Day'.[15]

In 1803 Coleridge was thinking about the problem of evil, but the approach he made to it changed dramatically because of an experience in May 1804. He was on board ship in the Mediterranean travelling to take up an appointment as the private secretary to Sir Alexander Ball, the Governor of Malta, when he suffered the intense misery that can result from sea-sickness. In a short while occurred the climax and summary of the previous years of illness and disappointment. Guilt was never a strong force in Coleridge, and it needed actual physical suffering to bring home the severity of pain and the gravity of the human situation. His youthful optimism had been fading, but it needed such an experience as this to lead him towards a totally new theodicy. He confided to his notebook his utter sense of helplessness as streaming through his mind went thoughts of 'the mere Passiveness with Pain (the essence of which is perhaps Passivity – & which our word – mere Suffering – well comprises –) in which the Devils are the Antithesis of Deity, who is Actus Purissimus, and eternal Life, as they are an ever-living Death.'[16]

Coleridge was thirty-one when he came to this turning-point in his life. It is interesting to see that Newman was only a few months older when he almost died of typhoid fever whilst travelling in Sicily in 1833. Both men were away from the comfort of friends and both were greatly affected throughout their lives by these Mediterranean miseries. Newman was more articulate in interpreting his experience and came to regard it as a preparation for his future work in saving the Catholic character of the Church of England.[17] In contrast, Coleridge was scarcely conscious of the change in his own outlook, and he understood his suffering not as a call to crusading action in preaching and circulating tracts, but as a revelation of the moral and physical weakness of man.

Just before he left England Coleridge had been reading Erigena[18] and Plotinus[19] and for the moment he contented himself with

37

the Platonic doctrine that evil is *metaphysical* nothingness. In a note of April 1805 he took the approach of regarding suffering as the deprivation of reason and goodness and equated matter with disorder, passivity and death, as opposed to self-determinate form, action and reason. 'So akin to Reason is Reality.'[20] However, this nonsense was soon purged from his system when he realized that any theology is meaningless that totally contradicts experience. This led him to reject the notions of Platonist and Scholastic theology.

> Evil according to some of the Schoolmen, & to the Platonists, subsisting in negation: consequently the Devil himself may be painted too black, as the Proverb very profoundly observes, for Evil being negation, if he were all evil, he would be nothing at all, which is a contradiction in terms.[21]

Coleridge was a bold man to abandon the most intellectually satisfying way belonging to theology to explain the existence of evil, and his scorn of the idea of a personal devil meant that he had to strike new ground in explaining sin and atonement. Considering the three traditional theories of atonement as the basis of all atonement theology before 1800, we can say that this departure from the ranks of the Unitarians was also a denial of the Abelardian or example theory: a denial of the real worth of history sets Anselm beyond the bounds for him, and disparaging the devil as 'a sort of Obnoxious Premier or Vizir of Providence'[22] sets him against any idea of ransom.

So where is Coleridge to begin? To start with, he never attempted to explain non-moral evil, that suffering which stems from happenings in nature beyond our control. 'Instead, therefore, of troubling himself with this barren controversy', the wise man 'more profitably turns to inquiries to *that* Evil which most concerns himself, and of which he *may* find the origin'.[23] This is moral evil whose source Coleridge firmly pinpoints in the will. As he came to regard faith as God's regenerating of the will, so he understood original sin to be the result of man's continual misuse of this will. Through his own experiences illuminated by his reading of Luther and Pascal among others, he became at times overwhelmed by the gravity of original sin, or that evil which has its origin in the will. He moved right away from the Irenaean position later adopted by Schleiermacher, and would have been appalled to find him referring to 'the irrelevant idea of the penal desert of original sin'.[24]

However, although Coleridge entered the fold of Augustinianism, he differed from some of its main assumptions. Unlike his disciple F. D. Maurice, he rarely thought in terms of the whole human race, and refused to accept the Fall of Adam as an actual historical event. Human history as a whole was not the ground in which the drama of the Fall and Redemption was played out but merely a shadow of what takes place in the individual's will. Accordingly, Coleridge viewed Adam as representing universal man, who comes to a fallen state by the misuse of his will. 'It belongs to the very essence of the doctrine that in respect of Original Sin *every* man is the adequate representative of *all* men. . . . Even in Genesis the word Adam is distinguished from a proper name by an Article before it.'[25]

However, although Coleridge believed that all men have a tendency to sin, he was, as far as the bulk of his statements show, convinced that they always retain the possibility of willing good. Coleridge followed Kant's teaching that the subject of all ethics is the will. To us this seems obvious enough, and we can see little point in their efforts to establish the independence and significance of the human will. But it is so easy to forget that a Utilitarian ethic had saturated English culture, and William Paley had lent his prestige to its introduction into the heart of Anglican thinking. The implication of this situation is well summarised by Professor Basil Willey:

> . . . the eighteenth century felt a deep nostalgia, not for the Eden of theology, but for the State of Nature from which man had somehow departed. . . . According to venerable theory, at least as old as Aristotle, reinforced by Stoicism and Christianity, and now re-emphasized by Descartes and Locke, man's essential nature was his rational soul. The real State of Nature, then, as Locke had said, has the Law of Nature (which is the Law of Reason) to govern it, and man's affairs are rightly ordered only when his institutions correspond to the true theory of human nature.[26]

This strong tendency to identify moral man with natural man very often meant that there was little distinction between ethical conduct and prudence. From here it need hardly be said that such a utilitarian ethic minimized the sphere of the will's activity and indeed left little room for any concept of free-will. Against this basic premise of the Enlightenment system Kant argued that man as a moral being has a will bearing with it its own autonomy totally distinct from nature.[27] In order to be truly moral, said Kant, one must act not by motives of prudence or desire, but, rather, according to the categorical imperative. 'However many natural causes, however many sensory stimuli there may be, which drive me to *will* something, they cannot produce (my state of) *being under obligation*. . . .'[28] This categorical imperative is completely independent of nature and natural laws, and springs from within the individual man.[29] The distinction Kant made between ethics on the one hand, and mathematics and natural science on the other, is summed up by the famous differing of the practical from the pure reason.

Coleridge came to absorb this distinction into his own thinking. It took time for Coleridge to get away from the rationalist notion that salvation cannot depend on repentance and good works on the ground that this is incompatible with the concept of divine justice. 'A mysterious Doctrine,' he informed his audience at Bristol in 1795,' is never more keenly ridiculed, than when a man of sense who professes it from interested motives endeavours to make it appear consistent with Reason.'[30] From here it was a long journey to the point where he saw reason in a technical sense as that special faculty given by God to all men. The distinction of the imagination from fancy preceded it by many years because Coleridge needed a theory of poetry, and Spinoza and Berkeley were already in his mind to provide it. He began to read Kant on his tour of Germany in 1799. But it was a slow process for it seems that he failed to assimilate the *Critique of Pure Reason* in any depth until that highly significant stay in Malta.[31] It was only in a letter of 1806 that he first spoke of 'the Reason and the Understanding . . . Vernunft, and Verstand.'[32] And it is but a short step until he recognises his real debt to Kant even though it is not until after 1815 that his theology flowers into a full bloom. 'I . . . am convinced that Kant in his Critique of the pure Reason . . . has completely overthrown the edifice of Fatalism, or causative Precedence as applied to Action.'[33] As the will becomes free from its bondage to prudence and rational considerations, man is once more given a vital part of himself that is at total liberty to move in the moral and spiritual realms. The will is so important, believed Coleridge, that without it any real faith is impossible. It alone determines whether or not a man, through his highest faculty, the reason, should enter into a personal act of faith, of which faith in Christ is the supreme example. In 1809 Coleridge made his second major attempt to produce a regular journal, *The Friend*. It contained much nonsense, but it heralded Coleridge's entry into theological maturity.

The feelings will set up their standard against the understanding, whenever the understanding has renounced its allegiance to the Reason; and what is faith, but the personal realization of the reason by its union with the will?[34]

Much else of Coleridge's later theology is a comment on this statement. Faith is reason raised to its highest key, that of the spiritual sphere. It is not only the highest faculty of spiritual perception, but also the precondition of regeneration. Thus, to summarise, faith is in essence the setting of the human will under the divine will, which can only be achieved by an act of the divine will. This takes the drama of fallenness and redemption, in which the human will is the principal character, right out of any contact with the rational world and sets it on a spiritual stage.

As Coleridge matured in his thinking he never ignored the fact that his own thoughts, like those of every person, must be seen against the background of their cultural setting. Every statement of consequence that he made shows its debt to some past thinker; every doctrine that he formulated was consciously put forward as part of some aspect of the broad European tradition of culture; even when he differed from some accepted teaching he rarely dismissed the traditional without a full explanation. Without having any real understanding of the nature of history and its development, he nevertheless revered the past and past thinkers of merit. This was the motive that led him to explain why he disagreed with that respected American divine, Jonathan Edwards Senior (1703-58), who 'attempted to raise the Calvinistic doctrine of determinism to the level of an inevitable metaphysic'.[35] In *Aids to Reflection*, which appeared in 1825 to become a manual of spiritual thinking for three generations of the more learned of England, Coleridge said that a man becomes 'in Christ'

> . . . not *by* Will of man alone: but neither *without* the Will. The doctrine of modern Calvinism as Laid down by Jonathan Edwards and Dr Williams, which represents a Will absolutely passive, clay in the hands of a Potter, destroys all Will. . . . It was in strict consistency therefore, that these Writers supported the Necessitarian Scheme, and made the relation of Cause and Effect the law of the Universe, subjecting to its mechanism the moral World. . . . [36]

Aids to Reflection spoke more about the subject of sin, redemption, and sanctification than any other of Coleridge's published writings. As he strove to interpret St Paul and especially St John,

41

the philosophy of Kant was often hovering in the background. Although he later modified his opinion, there is more than a grain of truth in the first impression it conveyed to that noted diarist and correspondent of Coleridge, Crabb Robinson. 'I . . . at first considered this as an attempt to express Kantian principles in the English language & adapt it to popular sentiment.'[37] The truth of the matter is simply that Coleridge found in Kant an understanding of the real character of man that England had never dreamed of. But he changed it from an intellectual monument of Germany into a servant for expressing the Christian doctrine of God to the English nation. God was no more the postulate of Kant's ethical system than of the mechanical universe of the deists. For Coleridge, as for his great inspirer, St John, God is the source of that reason 'which lighteth every man that cometh into the world'; he is the basis of all ethics; he 'is the Cohesion & the oneness of all Things – and dark & dim is that system of Ethics; which does not take 'oneness' as the root of all Virtue.'[38] So wrote Coleridge when he commented on that most English of poets, John Donne. Indeed it is a testimony to the perceptive nature of Coleridge that he saw the elements in Kant's work that would be of assistance in allowing the English tradition to gain more power of expression and never bothered the general reader with the rest.

Very often the French or German writer has been ready to publish only the distillate of his thought with many of the self-contradictions removed. Coleridge expresses his Englishness in taking his reader through the meanderings of his mind, and nowhere does he do this more obviously than in facing the perennial problem for the theologian of preserving the freedom of the will in the presence of the grace of God. At one point in *Omniana* of 1816 he states categorically that the individual is entirely responsible for the way in which he uses his will, and yet only two pages later says he is only capable of moral evil, which was inherent in the will from the time of birth.[39] This is a fact that he never attempted to mollify. We have seen the effect that Coleridge's understanding of his own weakness and failings had on his earlier thinking. This same sense of failure haunted his later years when he was so dependent on the hospitality and medical supervision of Dr Gillman at Highgate. His personal feelings at this time come to the surface when J. H. Green and others of his well-wishers proposed to settle an annuity on him. 'Can I do it without moral degradation? And . . . can it be done without loss of character in the eyes of my acquaintances and of my friends' acquaintances?'[40] And so conscious of his own weakness of will, he frequently used his private notebooks to elaborate upon the view that this is the seat of moral evil.[41] Only when he had achieved some degree of clarity did he make public his thoughts in *Aids to Reflection*.

Evil, he decided is an empirical fact, which we apprehend by the 'Law of Conscience' and our 'Responsible Will'.[42] There is a moral evil common to all men 'and this evil must therefore have a common ground'. This evil ground cannot have its origin in the Divine Will, and he has already rejected the traditional idea of the Devil where evil is a *unified*, personal power. Consequently Coleridge is theoretically left with two possible alternatives, the first of which is to postulate a God limited in either power or benevolence. With the exception of a very few such as Hastings Rashdall at the beginning of this century, who thought that God was still working towards omnipotence, this has not been the way of the Christian theologian. To one so deeply Christian as Coleridge, the only path is to face the problem of sin in its most ultimate and difficult form. This he does not flinch from doing, and concludes that the basis of moral evil 'must . . . be referred to the Will of Man. And this evil Ground we call Original Sin'.[43]

Here is the divergence between Coleridge as a man and Coleridge as a thinker. The former was often weak, but the latter had the courage to face head on the two most difficult problems confronting anyone who sets out to account for the existence of wickedness in the presence of the Christian God. *First, how can man be said to have a totally free will when he is only capable of evil? Secondly, why does the all-powerful and benevolent God allow the situation to develop and continue whereby moral evil is perpetually being created?*

We are in the first of these back to the old problem of grace and free-will. As Coleridge grew in his knowledge of Martin Luther it seems justifiable to wonder whether in his mature period after 1815 the Reformer's ideas helped him in tackling this problem from a specifically Christian standpoint. At this time 'the old thin folios of Martin Luther's *Table Talk* translated by Captain Henry Bell with Laud's sanction and approval . . . seems to have lain nearer to Coleridge's heart than any other book except the Bible.'[44] Indeed with the exception of Coleridge's admirer, Archdeacon Julius Hare, no Englishman in the early nineteenth century was a greater student of his.[45] As Coleridge became more and more interested in theology, we should expect Luther to stimulate his thinking on this perennial problem of grace and freewill. But he still preferred Kant for giving man an independent will. Any notion Luther or Calvin might have had of the infinite goodness and power of God overpowering the human will was not acceptable to Coleridge. Coleridge had spent a number of years in extracting man from the rationalists' mechanical and deterministic system; he now had no intention of letting him lose his autonomy in any theological edifice. This is the thinking behind a paragraph in *Notes on Luther's Table Talk:*

> . . . confounds free-will with efficient power, which neither does nor can exist save where the finite will is one with the absolute Will. . . . In fact, till the appearance of Kant's *Kritiques* of the pure and of the practical reason, the problem had never been accurately or adequately stated, much less solved.[46]

Coleridge never saw much difference between the positions of Calvin and Luther. Indeed he had a great respect for Calvinism and much preferred it to Arminianism on account of the assurance it provides for the believer. But because of his sensitivity to the faith of others, he is very reticent to speak of the most famous Arminian, who had won the hearts of some of the poorest of the nation, John Wesley. Instead, he forms his thought by criticising one whom he loved more, but others knew little, namely that saintly seventeenth century Irish bishop, Jeremy Taylor. 'If ever a book was calculated to drive men to despair, it is Bishop Jeremy Taylor's on Repentance. It first opened my eyes to Arminianism, and that Calvinism is *practically* a far, far more soothing and consoling system.'[47] All in all, Coleridge found no satisfactory statement of what is meant by the freedom of the will in any of the classical theologies. He properly saw this as one of the really great achievements of Kant, who gives us one of the best summaries of his thought in the *Metaphysic of Morals*:

> What else then can freedom of the will be but autonomy, that is the property of the will to be a law to itself? But the proposition: The will is in every action a law to itself, only expresses the principle, to act on no other maxim than that which can also have as an object itself as a universal law. Now this is precisely the formula of the categorical imperative and is the principle of morality, so that a free will and a will subject to moral laws are one and the same.[48]

Kant has in this last sentence especially stated the paradox of the free-will and the moral law. He could not solve the problem, for it will never be solved. But unlike anyone before him, he did set forth the issue without depriving man of his will. This is the appeal he had for Coleridge, who took Kant's interpretation of religion out of the ethical key and raised it to the spiritual through making his 'reason' God-centred. This is not one of the simpler parts of Coleridge's theology; however, to put this in a different way, when God reveals himself to a particular person, he enables his will to place itself under the divine will. It is then in harmony with the 'reason', which God gives to all men, and the product of the two is faith. This does not give an intellectual solution to the problem of sin and free-will, for such a solution would belong to the sphere of the understanding and is therefore impossible to provide. However faith does give us a more important answer, and one that is pertinent to the needs of sinful men, for it leads to regeneration. 'Faith essential to Regeneration. For Faith is the marriage of the Will and the Reason: or shall I call it the offspring of that Union?'[49] Redemption is Coleridge's answer to the problem of sin, and, like Luther's, it is an 'Augustinian' answer. In redemption God *rectifies* the fallen state of man.

But here as in his personal life Coleridge shows the same double-mindedness. He wanted to be rid of the habit of opium, but looked back on what had happened before. He marred his public lectures by thinking of all his past failures, and so was it true of his theologising. He so often prepared his readers for a statement of the Christian doctrine of redemption, but is haunted by his sense of failing to give an adequate explanation of what sin is. And so he retraces his footsteps and we become involved in his old trap of an over-complex metaphysic. However to be fair, this is one of the areas in which his philosophising has a very modern ring about it. The precise nature of evil the Continental Reformers were prepared to ignore and see dissolve in the process of redemption. This could now satisfy the speculative mind of Coleridge who wanted a 'general theory of the nature of evil such as Augustine offered in his privative analysis, his use of the principle of plenitude, and his conception of the aesthetic perfection of the universe.'[50] It was to Platonism that Coleridge turned in his continual effort to find a satisfactory formal statement of the origin of moral evil. He played with his ideas in his later private notebooks,[51] and generally the reasoning went something like this. The seat of moral evil is the will. The right course for the will to adopt is to set itself under the divine Will, where it has no form of its own, but is subsumed under the Form of the Supreme Good. Where the will asserts itself apart from the Divine Will, the potential evil in the human will takes on an independent form and thus becomes positive evil. Evil is essentially disunity: therefore form must be borrowed from Good in order that positive evil can come into existence at all.

Pure evil can never exist, because this is what the evil will *alone* would manifest without form derived from Good. Evil form is a contradiction in terms. The view that disunity is evil is an important discovery, which we shall see more of when we look at Coleridge's theory of the personality. However, we are led to the former conclusion that all Coleridge's efforts to express Christian theology in a closed Platonist system entails unnecessary confusion.

Coleridge seemed to have realised that the general public could not absorb all this. So in his *Aids to Reflection* he told his readers that original sin and the Christian doctrine of redemption can only be explained in terms of each other. 'The doctrine of Original Sin concerns all men. But it concerns Christians *in particular* not otherwise than by its connection with the doctrine of Redemption; and with the Divinity and Divine Humanity of the Redeemer as a corollary or necessary inference from both mysteries.'[52] This is terribly important, for it shows that Christology was for Coleridge not something to be considered apart from the doctrine of salvation, but inherently bound together with it. Patristic Christology and traditional theories of Atonement were of little interest to him, for they rested on the assumption that the two could be considered as almost independent segments of Christian theology. Coleridge heralded the modern era in setting nearly all his thinking on the Person of Christ in the context of its effect on the individual believer. It is only in the last fifty years that the English tradition has come to treat the office and person of Christ as belonging so closely together, and even the best of those who loved Coleridge's teaching, Maurice and Westcott, failed to see the significance of his approach. Dr Wolfhart Pannenberg has attributed the distinction to Schleiermacher, and the fact that they belong to a similar place in cultural history with the Romantic stress on the value of the individual, his soul and awareness, that led to them making this same breakthrough in the development of theology.[53]

However, this does not mean that Coleridge was not indebted to those before him. Rather the opposite is the case. He was conscious of his theological heritage more than any Englishman before him. And it showed the calibre of his mind that he was prepared to make himself an heir of the Continental Reformers. Indeed he believed that Luther is the almost perfect interpreter of St Paul,[54] and agreed with him by the time he came to write *Aids to Reflection* that rather than analyzing the present situation, it is much more fruitful for us to look forward to our future as redeemed persons. This is more clearly apparent in a note on Luther's *Table Talk*.

Luther: When Satan saith in thy heart, God will not pardon thy sins, nor be gracious unto thee, I pray (said Luther) how wilt thou then, as a poor sinner raise up and comfort thyself, especially when other signs of God's wrath do beat upon thee, as sickness, poverty, &c. . . .

Oh! how true, how affectingly true is this! . . . But the Gospel answers – 'There is a redemption from the body promised; only cling to Christ. Call on him continually with all thy heart and with all thy soul, to give thee strength and be strong in thy weakness; and what Christ does not see good to relieve thee from, suffer in hope.[55]

What precisely is the benefit of the saving work of Christ? As we have seen, for the present life Coleridge saw it as a reintegrating of the personality. This was his lifelong belief from the earliest poems to the latest notebook entries. Here was a vital move from Rationalism into Christian Romanticism; here was the experience of a man who knew the reality of God apart from the hypothesis of the deistic world-view.

With even more significance than this, Coleridge gave new life to the traditional Christian doctrine of a future life achieved by the Atonement of Christ. Theology had been plagued in the eighteenth century by the rationalist tenet that Jesus was the teacher who explained that 'future rewards and punishments' were the direct result of actions in this life. This was the tradition which was given its classical English form by John Locke and persevered into the nineteenth century. But his reading of Luther led Coleridge back to the mediating Christ of St Paul and to interpreting Christ's future benefits in terms of the Credal affirmation: 'I believe in . . . the Resurrection of the Body.'

Here he brought to bear the new higher criticism of the Bible that he had become acquainted with through his knowledge of happenings in Germany, and realised that St Paul's mature teaching was that of the first Corinthian epistle and not the cruder eschatology of Thessalonians. Here the Apostle 'substitutes the doctrine of immortality in a celestial state and a spiritual body.'[56] The afterlife, perceived Coleridge, will be a new life in a new and spiritual body. To us this sounds obvious, but to one living at a time when apologetic rested on the supports of the arguments from design, prophecy and miracle as set forth by Paley and Watson, it was an achievement to ignore the great attention paid to Jesus's raising of people from the dead! Coleridge was a member of a Church of England which could look a long way ahead to J. B. Mozley's defence of the old rationalist appeal to 'Miracles' in his

Bampton Lectures of 1865, and had a generation still to run before F. D. Maurice was to lose his chair for suggesting in his *Theological Essays* that future punishment is not everlasting and that *aionios* in the New Testament has no connotation of an endless chronology.

Now this latter is most interesting. Maurice was one of that gifted circle of young men, which included John Sterling, John Stuart Mill and Connop Thirlwall, who used to visit Coleridge in his last years at Highgate merely to hear his long discourses on subjects theological and political. It was here that Maurice 'was to imbibe his eschatological ideas',[57] which he in turn was to pass on to Charles Kingsley[58] and F. W. Farrar, a pupil at King's College. But what was it that Coleridge himself thought? The first occasion which showed the direction in which his mind was moving was in a letter which Coleridge wrote in April 1814 to his friend, benefactor and former publisher, Joseph Cottle. Here he expresses some doubt as to whether the Scriptures do teach that some will not be saved, and even if they will not be saved, whether they will suffer everlasting punishment.

> As to eternal punishments, I can only say that there are many passages in Scripture, and these not metaphorical, which declare that all flesh shall be finally saved; that the word *aionios* is indeed used sometimes when eternity must be meant, but so is the word 'Ancient of Days', yet it would be strange reasoning to affirm, that therefore the word ancient must always mean eternal. The literal meaning of *aionios* is, 'through ages'; that is indefinite; beyond the power of imagination to bound.[59]

Coleridge was sufficiently discreet to keep his observations on this question to his own deliberations and private correspondence. In this same letter he says that 'as to the effects of such a doctrine, . . . it would be more pious to assert nothing about it, one way or the other'. But it was not only his admirable respect for public belief and popular piety, with its widespread Calvinistic assumptions, that prevented Coleridge from giving the question a public airing. His thinking on the Election-Universalism issue was never clarified, and he contented his mind with a mention in *Aids* of a sympathy for those who cannot reconcile the idea of election with their moral feelings.[60] However, the very fact that he was aware of the problem showed him to be alive theologically, which is more than can be said for most of the Church of England in the early part of the last century, and when we consider how many theological traditions found a home in his mind we ought not to be surprised at uncertainty over some matters. Only a very rare man could have drunk deeply at Luther and Calvin's wells of riches, whilst contemporaneously admiring the Quakers of the seventeenth and early eighteenth centuries, who 'believed in the possibility of universal salvation', [61] and still had an unshakable opinion.

Although it was in his private letters and conversations with his admirers, the advancedness of Coleridge's notion that *aionios* need not mean 'everlasting' is sufficiently indicated by the fact that another man could lose a university chair for expressing the same thing in a single essay forty years later. Superficially it is not difficult to see why Maurice was condemned and Coleridge ignored. *Essays and Reviews* was to show how vulnerable a clergyman with dangerous opinions was compared with a layman, and in any case no one would bother with an eccentric and unemployable dreamer as Coleridge was regarded by the educated public of the day. On a deeper level the difference is indicative of the two generations. Maurice worked at a time when events such as the Oxford Movement and the Gorham case had made the Church of England alive to matters of theology, whereas in the early part of the century rationalism, combined with a general laxness, had produced a situation to which the missionary and social awareness of the Evangelicals and the Hackney Phalanx gave sparse relief. In his knowledge of the Scriptures, and every other theological discipline apart from the Old Testament languages, Coleridge has no comparison among his English contemporaries. Here we have another case where he could have saved a generation of effort, but no man without any ability to harness his talent is ever given a hearing.

For all this, we would be wrong to suppose that in this aspect of his teaching, as in many others, Coleridge was a Melchisedek, isolated from any tradition and without a precursor. Dean Farrar, as we have seen, himself a follower of Maurice, reckoned that Coleridge found a similar limitation upon the idea of eternal in Jeremy Taylor.[62] Farrar also points out that certain of the Fathers, including Augustine and Gregory of Nyssa used the word in a sense other than meaning 'endless'.[63] Here we have another sign of the secret of Coleridge's greatness. What at first sight appears to be a most radical idea in the development of theology has its mainspring in his ability to explore and evaluate the work of great minds of the past whom his English contemporaries had either forgotten, or had not the application and linguistic and philosophical knowledge to approach. And the easiest mistake to make in groping towards the heart of Coleridge's work is not to recognise a deeper level in him than a mere ability to marshal the ideas of others. His use of these ideas was expressive of a man of his conviction and his time. And for Christians in England in the first half of the nineteenth century the overriding concern was with the state of their souls and eternal salvation. It is obvious in Tractarians such as Newman and Hurrell Froude, and in Evangelicals such as Wilberforce. Their statements cry out with their inward fears. In contrast, Coleridge's writings so often mask this great concern by their intellectual framework and dress. But it is there none the less, and shown by the fact that as far as possible he places the action of redemption of the Word and Spirit in the inward soul in the here and now. To this end the theology of Luther and the metaphysic of Kant were useful aids; but they were never the inspiration of Coleridge's prime conviction, only suitable expressions of it.

Thus we have a tension between Coleridge's stress on disclosure in the here and now and, on the other hand, the significance the whole Christian tradition has placed in the historical figure of Jesus Christ in achieving the possibility of salvation by the events of Calvary and Easter. We shall look at this problem in detail in the next chapter, but we can say that it haunted Anglican theology in the last century. Bishop Russell Barry well observed that even at the end of the century the individual humanity of Jesus and the historical character of his work was being played down by stressing the 'Antiochene' Christology to an extreme degree. Coleridge heralded by writing of the Word's 'incomprehensible Goodness of Deity in taking upon himself *Man*, in order to incorporate, or rather inspirituate, Man into himself –'.[64] We may find this a serious weakness, but in the prevailing cultural climate he could do no other. In England Paley's rationalist approach left little room for revelation through history, and Kant and Lessing totally divorced theology from particular events. At least he was aware of the problem where many even in the following generation, F. D. Maurice among them, seemed largely oblivious to it. Maurice and his friends gave England a Christianity without the suffering individual humanity of Jesus while the Germans were seeking for Jesus at the expense of the transcendent. Coleridge did better than either in attempting to overcome the dilemma by regarding the Crucifixion and Resurrection as symbolical of the regeneration of every Christian, and also as realizing the possibility of redemption. In *Omniana* Coleridge says of Jesus Christ that 'his crucifixion, death, resurrection, and ascension, were all both symbols of our redemption (φαινόμενα τῶν νουμένων) and necessary parts of the aweful process'.[65] Although we shall see that history cannot be dissolved in metaphysics, Coleridge deserves much credit for seeing the difficulty much in advance of any other Englishman.

Another important contribution Coleridge made to the theology of redemption was his revival of the doctrine of sanctification. With the exception of such as the Quakers and early Methodists in England, and the Moravians in Germany, since the initial thrust by the great figures of the Reformation this was an area to which Protestant theology had given little attention. Then at the turn of the last century new winds began to blow. In the philosophy and poetry of Romanticism was an intellectual framework sympathetic to the expression of the deepest religious emotion. Kant and Schleiermacher were influenced by Moravian Pietism more deeply than they may have imagined, and, with the Kant-Lessing revolution's stress on the inward man, gave rise to a wide interest in personal religion and holiness, which demanded a theological statement of what is meant by sanctification. The Evangelicals and the Methodists were making a similar move in England; but whereas they were ecclesiastical, the Germans were academic; whereas they went straight to the Bible, Schleiermacher stressed apologetic and contemporary culture. Only Coleridge combined the two attributes of being both an Englishman and a man of intellectual substance. This was to reap its reward in his ability to influence the next generation of divines. In a manner characteristic of the English approach to theology he went straight to the Bible. But in order to interpret what it says on santification he used his great perception of theological tradition, and so it is in his 'Notes on Luther's Table Talk' that we find the heart of his teaching.

> . . . surely, justification and sanctification are one act of God, and only different perspectives of redemption by and through and for Christ. They are one and the same plant, justification the root, sanctification the flower; and (may I not venture to add?) transubstantiation into Christ the celestial fruit.[66]

This is the most poetic statement of a belief that sanctification is to be seen alongside justification as the completion of a single process. This is typical of Luther's teaching and to us does not seem remarkable. But it was novel for England to have a man thinking seriously about the heart of theology, namely the doctrine of Atonement, when for a century it had had little better than the solely devotional material of William Law, the enthusiasm of the field preachers, and the polemic of Bishop Warburton which opposed this latter group. Now Coleridge added his own stamp to his expression of sanctification, giving it a dynamic interpretation which is so characteristic of the Romantic's understanding of the whole of life. It is not merely a dogmatic conception, but a process that we can experience, and it is what Coleridge is writing of in one of his letters:

> Now that state which is selfish; yet not wholly selfish, not virtuous yet not wholly without virtue, is the Intermedium that makes it possible to pass from Vice to Holiness.[67]

As we come to the specific task of giving historical perspective to Coleridge's work on the Atonement we have to set it against an age which outside Methodist and Evangelical circles saw it as no more than guaranteeing a future existence where rewards and punishments would be handed out according to deserts. Joseph Priestley was not untypical when in his *History of the Corruptions of Christianity* (1782) he wrote that 'the great object of the mission and death of Christ' was 'to give the fullest proof of a future life of retribution, in order to supply the strongest motives to virtue.'[68] Even within the Church of England there was very little of the feeling of the depravity of man and his need for personal salvation which Coleridge's understanding of himself provided. Even Bishop Butler's view of man is too clouded by Enlightenment optimism in comparison with the mature Coleridge, for

> . . . whereas Butler thinks merely of human sin, so far as it entails future punishment and of redemption as remission of penalty, Coleridge thinks of it as a depravation of the will itself, and of redemption as regeneration.[69]

Coleridge was the first major religious thinker to be totally discontented with the shallow optimism and its ensuing doctrine of man to which so much of the eighteenth century had adhered. His exact German contemporary F. D. E. Schleiermacher, who occupied a similar place in the history of German theology as he did in England and has always been far more celebrated in theological circles, had a very different understanding of the nature of human life. Personal guilt was something that meant much less to him than to Coleridge, and this led him to a very different understanding of the place of the Atonement. There has been a tendency to assume too great a similarity between the two, such as we find in R. S. Franks's statement that 'both make redemption by Christ the centre of Christianity, and identify redemption with regeneration. English theology, therefore, through the influence of Coleridge enters on the same career as that of Germany through the influence of Schleiermacher.'[70]

This is plainly contrary to fact. After Schleiermacher German theology devoted itself to the two tasks of examining the historical character of the Bible and subjecting God to the ramblings of various versions of Hegelian metaphysics. In contrast, the principal followers of Coleridge were doctrinal and pastoral, with people like Hare, Maurice and Kingsley pursuing the task Coleridge began of interpreting the cardinal teaching of the New Testament and the Reformers to the souls of the people of England. That brilliant English divine and writer of that penetrative essay on *Coleridge* in 1856, F. J. A. Hort, lived too near in time to see the historical perspective. But he was the only person who has clearly stated that Coleridge differed from Schleiermacher in his belief about the *significance* of the Work of Christ because of their radically contrary understanding of the gravity of sin and man's plight through it.

> . . . the scornful experience of his own (i.e. Coleridge's) inward life had been for him, as for St Augustine, a source of another kind of light than any which speculation could supply. The consciousness of evil, born with him and clinging to him, was brought home to him with a power and a clearness which made all sentimental dallying with the matter impossible. This is one of the fundamental points in which his theology stands in the sharpest opposition to that of Schleiermacher, with which it is sometimes ignorantly confounded. Monstrous as it seemed to him to give the name of evil to much that is only a lesser and lower kind of good, he thought that all falsehood lies in calling evil only a lesser good.[71]

Thus Hort rightly observed that Coleridge had a far greater perception of the fallenness of man than Schleiermacher, and that he saw redemption as the direct rectification or the only medicine for the human plight. Indeed Schleiermacher himself knew that in the Christian tradition there is one kind of theology which stresses the difference between man's present state and his created perfection, and another which minimizes the difference. 'It may . . . be said that in the development of the Church's doctrine there has been an almost constant wavering between these antagonistic positions.' These he respectively termed 'Manichaeism' and 'Pelagianism' which are the extreme positions of what John Hick has termed the Augustinian and Irenaean traditions of theodicy.[72] Unlike

Coleridge in his mature phase, Schleiermacher unquestionably belongs to the latter category, and his theodicy is one of Hick's main themes. 'Man's own original perfection . . . is . . . for Schleiermacher, not a primordial and long-since-forfeited condition of human virtue but the structure of human nature whereby "in our clear and waking life a continuous God-consciousness as such is possible".'[73] To put this another way, whilst Coleridge was restating the Augustinian-Lutheran doctrine of the Fall, Schleiermacher was making the common objection that this entails one of two serious objections. The more one ascribes responsibility to Satan, the less free will there can be. On the other hand, if the freedom of the will be stressed, sin can only be viewed as the result of some inherent evil in man. It does not require much imagination to see the disapproval Schleiermacher would have given Coleridge for accepting the inherence of evil in man, along with the doctrine of the Trinity, as one of the axioms of Christianity which cannot be debated about but only believed.

Yet for all their knowledge of Schleiermacher, all of the great liberal English divines of the last century preferred to follow the less intellectual but more traditional theodicy of Coleridge.[74] One significant reason for this was that in Britain theology was seen almost exclusively as the servant of the Church with its primary function to expound the Scripture and the traditional doctrine to the nation. In contrast to Germany, where theology always tends to academic isolation, scholars in England generally started from the positions which most people assumed. We have only to mention the incidents over Maurice's teaching on eternal life and the early debate on evolution to see the stir which happened when they did not. Theologically the most significant of Coleridgeans were Julius Hare, F. D. Maurice, and F. J. A. Hort, and through his influence on them, Coleridge ensured that English theology retained a far greater hold upon the reality of sin, the fallenness of man and the redemptive mercy of God than its German counterpart.

Maurice had read Coleridge before he went up to Cambridge,[75] whereas there is no evidence to suggest that he had any real knowledge of Schleiermacher's work until he came to prepare for the writing of his *Moral and Metaphysical Philosophy*, which appeared in 1862.[76] The other great influence on Maurice's earlier thinking on the Work of Christ was that strange Scottish recluse, Thomas Erskine (1788-1870), who, after initially practising law, spent most of his life in obscurity on his estate at Linlathen studying theology. Maurice read his book, *The Brazen Serpent* (1831), in the year of its publication,[77] and formed a favourable opinion of it. It seems probable that his idea of the redemption of Christ 'to declare the race partaking of that nature forgiven, and to lay up in him, their glorious Head, eternal life for them all'[78] led to Maurice's own teaching of Christ as 'the Head and King of our Race'. But it was Coleridge, especially through *Aids to Reflection*, who more than any other imprinted on Maurice's mind the Augustinian doctrine of the fallenness of man and his need of restoration through Christ. This was the tradition of the great Reformers, and it is significant that Maurice clearly associated Coleridge with Luther when speaking of the redemptive sacrament of Baptism in his dedicatory letter to Derwent Coleridge, prefaced to the second and subsequent editions of *The Kingdom of Christ*.[79] Maurice was a man of a different cast from Coleridge, Newman, Robertson of Brighton, and many others of the age who lived more within themselves, and were governed by bouts of depression and a perpetual fear for their souls. Halfway between them and the rugged outlook of Kingsley, he lived in the more practical realm of social concern, educational ventures, teaching and pastoral work. Nevertheless, he was sensitive to the needs of Englishmen, and his beautiful essay 'On the Atonement' explains redemption with great clarity as simply the removal of sin and the restoration of a former relationship with God. His very use of the Johannine word 'Advocate' would seem to indicate that he saw the Work of Christ as a restoration of a previous relationship, and not a further step in the soul-making process.[80] We get strong echoes of *Aids to Reflection*, which Maurice so much admired, where original sin and redemption are seen in terms of a severance and subsequent reconciliation of the human will with that of God. In addition to this, Maurice was truly drawing on the heart of Coleridge's teaching when he adopted the view that sin and redemption is something that happens to the will of man. This is nowhere clearer than in an essay 'On the Evil Spirit', when he writes of 'an Evil Spirit whose assaults are directed against the Will in man'.[81]

Although Maurice did more than anyone else in the long term to gain recognition for the Coleridgean way of approaching theology, he only whispered what Julius Hare, 'a more devoted Coleridgean than Maurice', shouted. In his primary work on the Atonement, *The Victory of Faith*, Hare has a vice-like grip upon Coleridge's axiom that it is the will which causes man's involvement in the drama of fallenness and redemption, and in broad terms we can say that he used Coleridge to restate Luther's doctrine of Justification by Faith. He clearly viewed the Fall as the fragmentation of man's personality through the corruption of the will, and faith as the state of the reintegrated personality achieved by an act of the will.

> While our Conscience, our Understanding, our Affections, and our carnal Appetites are dragging us in opposite directions, the Will is torn and mangled, and almost dismembered: and from this misery nothing can save us, except the atoning power of Faith.[82]

Hare's book was frequently to be found in the libraries of the clergy and more thoughtful laity and was important in mediating to a wider public a religion which was thoroughly Christian and yet avoided the stress of the Tractarians on ecclesiastical authority on the one hand, and the labour of the Evangelicals' emotionalism on the other. Of all the Victorians no one was more thoroughly an Anglican than Hare: respect for the Church's authority, yet not subservience; a love of tradition, yet no fear of looking to the present implications of the past; deepest concern for clear thinking, yet an avoiding of over-intellectualizing the religious inward element out of religion; all these were combined in one person.

Yet Hare had a chink in his intellectual armour which was to prevent him being an ideal interpreter of Coleridge. Those who share the prevalent view that in his latter years at Highgate Coleridge just held forth to the young men who visited him with a monologue that was totally unaware of the capacity of the listener will need to revise their opinion. In spite of all he had to say on the distinction between the reason and the understanding, it was Hare of all his hearers that stood out in his mind as missing the point. When he was commenting on a sermon of John Donne, he doubtless had in mind an early and subsequently popular joint production with his brother. 'Faith seems to me the co-adunation of the individual Will with the Reason. . . . Till this distinction (of Reason and Understanding . . .) be seen, nothing *can* be seen aright. Yet Mr Hare writes of it as a sort of arbitrary repr. in words much like *sweat* and *perspire*. . . . So little had he comprehended me.'[83] *Guesses at Truth* had failed to guess the heart of Coleridge's teaching.

This is all part of the irony about Coleridge. He failed to project his brilliance himself, and this failure was hardly rectified in his most ardent admirers. Maurice used Coleridge but did not set forth the elder's claims with any conviction; Hare did his best but had his own limitations, and in the next theological generation the one who knew and loved his work best, F. J. A. Hort, with his ingrained reticence to publish anything, only managed a medium length contribution to the *Cambridge Essays* of 1856. This was excellent in itself, being praised by Leslie Stephen as 'the only serious attempt known to him to give a coherent account of Coleridge's philosophy'. Initially the drift of Coleridge's ideas percolated to Hort early in his life through his reading of Maurice and Hare, and it seems likely that he dipped into Coleridge before he went up to Cambridge and continued it until well into middle life. This whole approach to things ultimate drew Hort as a magnet, and although a shy young undergraduate he plucked up sufficient courage to actually visit Maurice who was then a professor at King's College, London. In fact he did all he could to catch the spirit of Coleridge, and *Aids to Reflection* was always one of the most used books in his library. 'It is quite unhistorical, and rambling and discursive in the extreme, but it is a book to be read again and again.'[84] On the subjects of the Fall, original sin, and predestination, Hort counted this one of the very great theological works, to be spoken of in the same breath as the classics of the great Reformers and Cambridge Platonists.

What is most interesting is that in 1848 at the age of twenty, a full decade before the name of Darwin was being breathed in college common-room or bishop's palace, Hort with his eyes open seized upon Coleridge's idea that the Fall of Adam was not a historical event, but rather stands as a 'type', representative of the fall of each individual. He expressed these thoughts in a letter to his close friend John Ellerton:

I am inclined to think that no such state as 'Eden' (I mean the popular notion) ever existed, and that Adam's fall in no degree differed from the fall of each of his descendants, as Coleridge justly argues that in each individual man there must have been a primal apostasy of the will, or else sin would not be guilty, but merely a condition of nature.[85]

Radical for its time as this may be, it is of minor import compared with the doubts Hort expressed to Maurice in the following year with regard to such entrenched and interrelated doctrines as a personal devil, eternal punishment and penal substitution. Especially with regard to the question of a personal devil, he said it 'was Coleridge who some three years ago first raised any doubts in my mind on the subject', but rued his failure to put the other view and attempt to see the advantages of the theory of penal substitution with its axiom of a personal devil.[86] However by 1860 he had no inhibition in telling his great friend Westcott that he regarded the doctrine of penal substitution as 'an immoral and material counterfeit' of the spiritual truth of Atonement.[87] This is typical of Coleridge's approach, but even thirty years after his death Hort, with his characteristic concern for the sensitivities of others, pointed out to the Bishop of Ely that his refusal to accept the traditional doctrine of Atonement might be a valid reason for not appointing him as an examining chaplain, a post which greatly attracted him.[88]

For all his indebtedness to Coleridge, we would be mistaken to believe that Hort's teaching on sin and Atonement did not differ from, and indeed, in many respects, have a richer content than that of the Sage of Highgate. Unlike Coleridge and Hare, he expressed sin and redemption as being more than almost solely the drama of the fallenness and subsequent regeneration of the human will. Hort's teaching on the Atonement is found in a concise form in his very important Hulsean Lectures, *The Way The Truth The Life*, which were delivered in 1871. At the appropriate point[89] he developed the theme that Atonement *commenced* with 'the sacrifice of the Cross', and continues in the Resurrection and the Work of the Holy Spirit, who imparts life to those who sacrifice themselves for the sake of him who is the Life. The stress on sanctification could only have been learnt from Coleridge; the element of sacrifice derived from Maurice.

So John Stuart Mill's observation has been well borne out. Coleridge was a 'seminal' thinker, and as such his theology percolated into the outlook of many important Anglican divines without stagnating into a school. This was because he made no claims for himself and he held no high office from which to build a theological empire. But in his presentation of the Atonement with all its accompanying issues he allowed much of the classical thinking to pass into forms that would not be out of place in the nineteenth century. There is little in Coleridge's teaching on Redemption that cannot be found in different language in St Paul and St John and Martin Luther. As we shall see, the more rigid criteria of philosophy and history gave him trouble in giving adequate weight to the historical Jesus. But it is in the field of teaching on personal redemption that the height of his theological influence was to be felt. He enabled this core of the Christian tradition to breathe in the same room as many of the intellectual giants of the first half of the English nineteenth century. With regard to his teaching on theodicy, sin and redemption, any of his disciples might have written what Neander said of Schleiermacher: 'From him a new period in the history of the Church will one day take its origin'.

4. Who was Jesus?

If we have the briefest glance at the Apostles' Creed we find at least two kinds of statement. There is first of all the type of affirmation which the believer thinks is permanently true and has a continuing effect on his faith. Then there are statements about God's revelation through the historical figure of Jesus. The two can be illustrated by the two articles 'I believe in the Holy Ghost', and 'Born of the Virgin Mary, Suffered under Pontius Pilate'. In both God reveals himself, but one influences us now directly and the other first took place in history. We might call the two personal disclosure and historical revelation. Coleridge was a genius in interpreting and explaining the first, but on the second he was sadly much weaker. This can be partially explained by the great difficulty every age has in explaining what it means by history; and the turn of the last century experienced a greater uncertainty than most periods because it marked a cultural upheaval from looking at history as facts to teach example to the early nineteenth century concept that history is some transcendent idea realizing itself in events. Thus Coleridge's understanding of history, like Mozart's music, stands on the brink between the Enlightenment and the nineteenth century. But whereas Mozart compelled himself to proceed deeper into the intricacies of his art, Coleridge found a reason whereby he could largely escape facing the difficult question over the character of history. Both in his thinking and everyday life there was a lack of courage at a crucial juncture which managed to prevent him achieving the greatest heights. And so he knowingly decided to ignore facts in theology as far as possible. He confided to his diary 'but for Christ, Christianity, Christendom, as centres of convergence, I should utterly want the *historic* sense. Even as it is, I feel very languid in all particular History.'[1] We can see how bad Coleridge was as a historian when even Maurice expressed this view. Strachey, Maurice's close friend, wrote to an aunt in 1836 that 'Maurice does not appear to me to be a great *reader*, though he has a far greater respect for facts than Coleridge had. He appears to consider this a great defect in Coleridge.'[2] Of

60

all the great Coleridgeans of his generation, Maurice had the worst grasp of history, treating the mythological and typological narratives of Scripture as if they were strictly factual. So a censure from Maurice was indeed a serious matter.

However no single man can be expected to pioneer in every field, and in Coleridge's time no Englishman was doing any profound work on the nature of history. In Germany one of the first to move away from the Enlightenment's deprecation of tradition with its refusal to recognize the contribution of past ages to the present standing of man was Johann Gottfried Herder. For Herder, to be human is not primarily to be a rational creature, as the eighteenth century generally believed. Rather, it is to live in history with all the experiences this provides. Although Crabb Robinson, ever friend, mentor and recorder of Coleridge during the latter part of his life, did visit Herder at his house in Weimar, there was no mediation of ideas that had any consequence. Indeed their views were directly opposite, for whereas Coleridge saw events as stemming from some metaphysical reality, Herder sought to evaluate facts as having complete validity within themselves. Applying this to the social sphere, 'Herder advocated reform from below whilst Coleridge addressed his *Manual* to the upper classes in the conviction that the reformation of English society must begin at the top.'[3]

Although Herder was not the man, it was a German who provided for Coleridge an intellectual justification for playing down the worth of history. As we have mentioned, his visit to Germany in 1798-9 gave an important impetus to his development. In the *Biographia Literaria* he tells us how he listened to eminent men in differing disciplines, from Blumenbach on physiology to Eichorn on the New Testament. But we can only agree with Hort that 'it was Lessing's work that affected him most powerfully at this time, as his letters clearly show.'[4] For example on 6th April 1799, Coleridge wrote to Thomas Poole, telling him that he was working very hard at Lessing. He intended to produce a proper published account of Lessing's life and work. This proceeded no further than a long rough draft in his notebook, but the important effect this study had on Coleridge is revealed to us in his conclusion that 'Lessing . . . was a most learned Historian, Theologist, & Orientalist – & deeply intent on purifying Religion from its prejudices.'[5] These 'prejudices' were the external evidences of the miracles of Jesus, the prophecies he fulfilled, and the argument that the intricacies of the universe demand that we postulate a designer. In other words, Coleridge found in Lessing good reasons for rejecting what he already detested in the English rationalist approach to theology. Lessing attacked the tremendous faith placed in the historical witness of Scripture. No one who does not personally witness an event can have total certainty of it. This applies to the resurrection of Christ; it cannot prove the permanent truth that he is the Son of God. We cannot, pleaded Lessing, jump this 'broad ditch' between fact and reason. In short, to use his own famous maxim, 'accidental truths of history can never become the proof of necessary truths of reason'.

Lessing's underlying motive for separating 'idea' and 'fact' was only revealed to his brother in a private letter. In the 1770's he had hoped to support orthodoxy against the rationalist theologians led by Semler so that he might clear the latter from the field before going on to destroy the whole of Christianity. It is ironical that although its logical fulfilment in Germany was D. F. Strauss's *Life of Jesus* (1835), which attempted to find behind the Gospel legends man's primitive hope for the resurrection of humanity as expressed in the myths about Jesus, in England it inspired Coleridge, permeated Newman's *Essay on Development* with its worship of idea and light regard for the value of the past, and in Denmark the famous maxim haunted Kierkegaard so much that it found its way to the title page of *Philosophical Fragments*.

We do not have to travel far to see the appeal that Lessing had for Coleridge. It is widely recognised that a Platonist is under a severe temptation to minimize the fact that Christianity stems from events that took place in space and time.[6] Coleridge gave a great amount of ground to this temptation as he attempted to put every facet of the Christian religion into one metaphysical edifice. Coleridge did not follow Lessing the whole way. But as we shall see, he managed to distort the doctrine of the Incarnation.

Yet many clouds have a silver lining. Coleridge, perhaps half unconsciously, found that a wedge between 'truth' and 'event' was an excellent weapon against the Paleyans. His reason for opposing Paley's argument from 'evidences' was very different from that which moved Lessing to undermine Semler's position. The last thing Coleridge wanted was the destruction of Christianity. Rather, he desired to state afresh the doctrines of St Paul, St John and Martin Luther, who all witnessed to a personal God revealing himself in the present time to those who have faith. So we can see how convenient it would have been for Coleridge to dismiss the 'evidences' as being of no consequence because of their belonging to the sphere of history.

In both England and Germany at the end of the eighteenth

century orthodoxy was replying to the rationalist, historical criticism with a rationalist and historical defence. In Lessing's view this would eventually result in revelation being subsumed under reason. In England Paley and Watson, and in Germany the neologians acted as though this time had already arrived. Lessing was alone in saying not yet. He realized they were doing justice to neither revelation nor reason. 'What a pity,' he said, 'nobody really quite knows where his reason or where his Christianity are.'[7] Lessing 'thought that . . . he was in agreement with the older theology, i.e. the orthodoxy of the sixteenth and seventeenth centuries, which was in the habit of presenting the historical proof only incidentally and without emphasis, and was not of the opinion that it could and should prove revelation as such by these means.'[8] To a foreigner unacquainted with all the intricacies of the German theological world, it would have appeared that Lessing was merely restating the Reformers' teaching that both the Church and the historical witness of the Bible were completely secondary in origin to the confession of faith, the *regula fidei*.

This is the thinking that coloured so much of Coleridge's theology, and is nowhere better illustrated than in a statement he made in 1806. 'Even as Christ did so would I teach; that is, build the miracle on the faith, not the faith on the miracle.'[7] Even more than this, Luther's maxim of *sola fide* was to haunt Coleridge throughout his life. As he began to read Luther on his German visit,[8] it seems a reasonable conjecture that he was led to him through his study of Lessing. It was convenient that Coleridge discovered at the same period Luther, who added dimension to his plan to interpret the Christian Religion mainly in terms of disclosure in the here and now and man's inward response, and Lessing, who helped his tendency to distrust history. This fits in with Coleridge's statement in the *Biographia* that after his early philosophical studies, which he was completing on his return from Germany, he sought to create a philosophical system as independent of history and its classifications as is at all possible.

> After I had successively studied in the schools of Locke, Berkeley, Leibnitz and Hartley, and could find in neither of them an abiding place for my reason, I began to ask myself: is a system of philosophy as different from mere history and historic classifications, possible?[9]

However this was to be an extreme position from which Coleridge soon withdrew. The external world meant far too much to him. The summer of 1800 found him beginning a four year stay in Keswick and becoming one of the first outsiders to experience and extol the sensuous splendour of the Lakeland majesty. As time went on, he resolved the conflict by treating the events of history as the concrete manifestations of principles.

> Standing midway between the eighteenth and nineteenth centuries, he shares in and combines what are generally taken as the leading characteristics of both, uniting the analytic and rational spirit of the one to the historical spirit of the other. As a poet and as a disciple of Burke, his natural tendency was to appeal to the facts of observation, to the sensual world of experience, and so to history. But as a student of the German Idealists, he had learnt to subordinate history to philosophy, and to discover in the historic process only the evolution of a philosophically conceived idea.[10]

Cobban is right. Coleridge stood in the mainstream of both the German and the English traditions. But from Burke he was given the necessary hint on how to preserve his conviction of the primacy of philosophy whilst at the same time paying his respects to history. We find the discovery in the *Biographia* where he was admiring Burke's treatment of history. 'Every principle contains in itself the germs of a prophecy; and as the prophetic power is the essential privilege of science, so the fulfilment of its oracles supplies the outward and (to men in general) the only test of its claim to the title.'[11]

This last sentence exactly describes Coleridge's attitude to the Jesus of history during the period of his maturity. He provides the outward guarantee of the truth of the 'ideas' of Christianity. The metaphysical remains the all-important, and Coleridge came to subsume the events of history under a metaphysical 'norm'. But facts still occupied a subordinate position, and just how subordinate was this position can be seen from two entries in the Table Talk belonging to the very end of Coleridge's life. 'After I had gotten my principles, I pretty generally left the facts to take care of themselves.'[12] As a footnote Coleridge added a passage from *The Statesman's Manual* of 1816 having a distinct ring of Lessing. 'The true origin of human events is so little susceptible of that kind of evidence which can *compel* our belief. . . .'[13] Coleridge himself was of the opinion that his conception of history had changed but little between 1816 and 1832.

The second entry in the *Table Talk* belongs to the end of 1831. It shows that Coleridge still had roots in the eighteenth century in *looking for* the 'lessons of history'.

If men could learn from history, what lessons it might teach us!
But passion and party blind our eyes, and the light which experience gives is a lantern on the stern, which shines only on the
waves behind us! [14]

From this we can see that Coleridge realized one cannot hope
for an 'impartial' history. Every writer of history carries his own
presuppositions and feelings into his subject. The one essential presupposition which Coleridge demanded of a historian is a philosophical one, which, in his view, should mould the facts without
neglecting such matters as historical evidence or chronology. This
lack of a 'philosophy of history' made Coleridge view Gibbon in a
most unfavourable light. 'Gibbon', he complained, 'was a man of
immense reading; but he had no philosophy; and he never fully
understood the principle upon which the best of the old historians
wrote.'[15]

The title of Coleridge's main work on political theory, *On the
Constitution of Church and State according to the Idea of Each*,
would in itself suggest that Coleridge evaluated these institutions,
as they stood in 1830, by the norm of the 'Ideas' he had of them.
This is precisely what happened. 'Scientific history', he wrote, is
'history studied in the light of philosophy.'[16] These 'Ideas' were
Coleridge's presuppositions. They were determined by what his
own peculiar brand of Toryism imagined the ideal Church and the
ideal State should be like. Employing this philosophical 'norm', he
lamented the fact that the burgesses elected landowners to Parlia-
ment: 'these things are no part of the Constitution, no essential
ingredients in the idea, but apparent defects and imperfections in
its realisation.'[17] We are now going to see that Coleridge treated
the Jesus of history in a similar way. He began with his own understanding of inward religion, and then proceeded to interpret the
historical events of Jesus's life in accordance with these 'Ideas' of
faith.

We now turn to consider how Coleridge interpreted the miracles
of Jesus. To the twentieth century reader this might appear a side
issue. But let him remember that even in 1865, six years after
the appearance of *Origin of Species*, that serious scholar J. B.
Mozley was so convinced of the importance of miracle as apologetic
that he defended it in his Bampton Lectures in the face of Darwin
and Huxley's virtual destruction of the idea of the universe as a
closed machine. In Coleridge's lifetime the majority of churchmen
rested content with Paley's restatement of the old deism of Derham
and Ray that miracle showed the presence of God in the self-

sufficient mechanism he had made. This was anathema to Coleridge who saw the world as a living and breathing organism. 'This is the philosophy of death, and only of a dead nature can it hold good.'[18] But it was not only the rationalist philosophy which was unacceptable to Coleridge. He found it difficult to accept the assumption that the Christian religion is based primarily on the historical activity of Jesus. On the other hand he was endowed with sufficient common sense to know that the whole life of Jesus, including his miracles, are an integral part of the traditional faith that it is inadmissible to rationalise them away in the manner of Eichorn.

> I do think it would be a proper punishment for my friend, Eichorn, to be made give an hypothetical history of the life of Christ from his Baptism to the Day of Pentecost, in which there shall be no *miracle*, and yet the facts introduced without the popular emotion about them – and the wonder, and Awe of the Apostles respecting their Master explained – so as they shall remain honest men without trick or guile.[19]

Coleridge's interest in miracle had begun in the early years of the new century when he had digested his reading of Spinoza, of whom he had great admiration as this note of 1803 amply shows. 'If Spinoza had left the doctrine of Miracles untouched, . . . his Ethics would never, could never, have brought on him the charge of Atheism.'[20] Indeed, in spite of his tendency to pantheism, Coleridge had to take notice of Spinoza as the only really great thinker of the Age of Reason who left room for a continuous relationship betwen God and the world he had made.

Spinoza also realised that without some *prior* knowledge of God, the Biblical miracles are not manifestations of his power and goodness: 'unless men are honestly endowed with the true knowledge and love of God, they may be as easily led by miracles to follow false gods as to follow the true God.'[21] In this Spinoza joined hands with Luther in leading Coleridge to the conviction that miracle is not the foundation of faith, as Paley had it, but solely a consequent. Now Coleridge saw miracle as both a concrete occurrence and a spiritual turning-point in the present day believer. This distinction was made by Luther in his *Table Talk* to which Coleridge was so attached.

> The visible and bodily wonders flourished until the doctrine of the gospel was planted and received, and baptism and the Lord's Supper established. But the spiritual miracles, which our Saviour Christ holds for miracles indeed, are daily wrought, and will

remain to the world's end, as that of the centurion, in Matt. viii, and that of the Canaanitish woman.[22]

In other words, Luther saw the centurion's acquisition of faith as a pattern of our gaining of faith in the here and now, which is the all-important 'spiritual' miracle. Coleridge took up this theme and viewed the pattern as the particular 'truth' that each miracle conveys to us. Thus the value of the miracle for the existential 'now' is for Coleridge the most important consideration of a miracle. In accordance with the rest of his theology, a miracle only becomes revelation when the eye of faith has perceived a correspondence between a present experience and the historical occurrence.

> . . . and especial blessing is attached to those whose belief of the Miracle is *consequent* on the perceived Correspondency and itself arises out of the Faith – so that instead of the belief in the Miracles being the occasion and actuation of the Faith, the Faith occasions and actuates the belief in Miracles.[23]

Therefore what took place in Palestine two thousand years ago only becomes a miracle because an individual in the present decides that for him it conveys an important spiritual 'truth'. That God chose to implant the pattern of this 'truth' in a concrete event was incidental as far as Coleridge was concerned. Corresponding to the way he placed secular history under a metaphysical 'norm', he regarded the miracles of Jesus as meaningful only by the existential 'norm' of faith. The facts are incidental to the 'truths' they illustrate. We now have to see whether Coleridge's view that their concrete form is incidental applies to his interpretation of the whole life of Jesus Christ on this earth.

For all his doubts, Coleridge fully accepted that in some way God had chosen to give the Christian religion roots in history. Indeed, he went far beyond this mere admission and spent considerable time keeping abreast of contemporary German study in the origins of Christianity, which is more than can be said of nearly all other Englishmen of the time. In preparing for the *Theological Lectures* of 1795 he almost certainly read a translation of Michaelis's *Introduction to the New Testament.* On his German tour, he attended Eichorn's lectures on the New Testament, and ten years later he informed his often perplexed wife that he was reading to their young son Hartley out of the latter's *Criticism of Esther.* By 1818 he had read sufficiently from the earlier writings of Paulus of Jena and of the works of the Old Testament scholar Rosenmuller and others to contemplate delivering a series of *critical* lectures on their achievements. It was not in the character of Coleridge to follow anyone's thought blindly, and these German 'neologists' served to stimulate him to a deeper study of the Gospels for himself.

This study soon produced the conclusion that the Gospels tell us very little of the factual occurrences of Jesus's life. He also perceived that there are several traditions in the Gospels, and very significantly concluded that St John has the weakest factual basis.[24] That he then proceeded to give it by far the greatest attention is some indication in itself of the importance he attached to the historical figure of Jesus. Coleridge came to believe that the Gospels are not essentially factual accounts, but rather statements of the *significance* of Jesus for the writers living some time after the events of Bethlehem to Pentecost. Just as we cannot simply take over the teaching of the past in our expression of what Jesus Christ means to us, neither could the Fathers of the fourth century or the Gospel writers of the first. The writers of all times have drawn far more upon their inward experience and conviction than upon empirical facts in their interpretation of the meaning of Jesus. This is what Coleridge was striving to express in this note.

> The improbability that all the articles of our Church & of the Universal Church in the 4 first centuries should have been abstracted from the Scriptures, & the Tradition of the Churches by men holding certain theoretical notions & grounding these articles thereon, & thereby defending them.[25]

It is easy from this to understand Coleridge's opposition to Eichorn's opinion that the chief aim of Gospel criticism and study should be to discern the primitive Gospel relating the facts about the ethical teacher Jesus of Nazareth, upon which the four evangelists built supernatural and idealizing embellishment. It was not Eichorn's method he objected to so much as the idea that Christianity can be explained in terms of an ethical teacher of the Socratic mould. 'Is it fitting,' he demanded of his host at dinner, 'to run Jesus Christ in a silly parallel with Socrates – the Being whom thousand millions of intellectual creatures . . . take to be their Redeemer, with an Athenian philosopher, of whom we know nothing except through his glorification in Plato and Xenophon?'[26] Jesus Christ must have been more than an ethical teacher for so many to rest their hope of salvation on him. So argued Coleridge when he confided to his notebook that the teaching of Jesus in

itself does not constitute a new religion for it is 'the mere extrica-
tion of the Moral Law of the Old Testament in reference to the
Individual from the political and ceremonial Ordinances binding
on the Jews, as members of a particular State'.[27] Thus, Coleridge
concluded that the Gospels show us that Jesus of Nazareth was
the founder of the movement called Christianity, which is of such
a kind that it cannot be explained by supposing him to have been
merely a great ethical teacher. He went beyond this and made it
quite clear that he thought the Gospels have a firm factual basis,
although the facts were not the leading interest of the writers and
became dominated by interpretation. For Coleridge the Gospels
were primarily the evangelists' expressions of the personal significance of Jesus Christ for them. From this they reflect certain
'truths' concerning man's redemption and relationship with God
that are important for all men regardless of the time or place in
which they live. God chose to use history as the medium in which
to reveal these 'truths'. But the fact that he used a man in Palestine
two thousand years ago has little religious meaning for modern
European man. Nevertheless, although he reckoned that it was
largely incidental that God established a spiritual religion through
a Jew of two thousand years ago rather than, for example, an
Indian of five thousand years ago, Coleridge accepted the fact that
he did.

This failure to understand why it was necessary for the Christ
event to have taken place within the context of the whole Jewish
tradition stemmed from a lack of sensitivity regarding the Hebrew
view of revelation. The Old Testament shows a continuing series of
related events in each of which God revealed something more of
his character. After a century and a half of further scholarship we
see Jesus Christ as a historical figure within this tradition giving
meaning to it, and at the same time through it being anchored in a
definite cultural situation. In contrast, Coleridge followed the
eighteenth century in showing a Jesus sadly devoid of the normal
human heritage of family and nation that determines to no small
degree the special character of each person. In the case of the
Jews, this tradition was a vehicle for God's revelation. Without
this idea, Coleridge could have had no reason to appeal to the
human features of Jesus. They could do nothing to show the
uniqueness of the event of Jesus Christ in giving rise to a spiritual
religion. In the *Table Talk* of April 13, 1830 Coleridge spoke of:

. . . that stupendous event – the rise and establishment of
Christianity – in comparison with which all the preceding Jewish

history is as nothing. With the exception of the book of Daniel, which the Jews themselves never classed among the prophecies, and an obscure text of Jeremiah, there is not a passage in all the Old Testament which favours the notion of a temporal Messiah. What moral object was there, for which such a Messiah should come? What could he have been but a sort of virtuous Sesostris or Bonaparte?[28]

We can only conclude that in comparison with the mainstream of the Christian tradition, Coleridge has seriously played down the revelatory significance of the human figure of Jesus. This was not his fault. One man cannot produce a revolution of thought in all spheres, and in regard to his treatment of history Coleridge was heir to an eighteenth century which saw no texture, no organic growth and interrelation, and little intrinsic value in the happenings of the past. Facts were material for the anvil of philosophy, both natural and moral. It is true that Coleridge replaced the philosophy of the English rationalists for that of Plato, Kant, and Lessing. Yet this alone could not allow him to escape from the habit of ignoring the particularity of each historical event which gripped the European mind. He interpreted the facts of Jesus's life by a metaphysical and 'spiritual' criterion. This had had little effect on English theology in the Enlightenment, for it largely avoided all consideration of Christology as the Fathers, the Schoolmen and the Reformers had struggled with it. God in creation had relegated God in redemption to nowhere. So when Coleridge took up the challenge to a truly Christian theologian, with salvation restored to its throne, he was bound to suffer from this vacuum. In connexion with the doctrine of the Incarnation, although he thought of Jesus Christ as fully human, he failed to conceive of him as being *a particular* man with his own peculiar characteristics. In his notebooks he justified himself by appeal to the Greek Fathers which in itself is remarkable in an England that had little interest in Church History and where advanced work in theology was confined to a minute number of scholarly men at the universities and cathedrals. In his maturity Coleridge thought that when the Logos was incarnate in the figure of Jesus, he was a 'symbol' of his own perfect spiritual existence as 'Idea'.

. . . if I am not mistaken, some of the Greek Fathers considered the Lord's assumption of Humanity as anterior to his Incarnation – He became Man, the *ideal* Man, before he became a Man. . . . In the Hebrew Commonwealth Christ became the Symbol of the *Unity* of the Nation . . . in condescending to reveal himself as the covenanted King of the Hebrews he made himself the Symbol of his own essential perfection.[29]

Here in his closing years we find Coleridge drawing the same parallel between the human mind and the nation as the one made later by Arnold and Milman, with just one exception. There is little notion of historical development in Coleridge. If in its history a nation remains fundamentally the same, so does its 'symbol' of unity. The 'symbol' is outside consideration of particular time. Just as a unified nation has its reason and will united, so does the integrated or redeemed human personality, which has the same 'symbol' as the Hebrew nation. Thus the Incarnation was for Coleridge just a manifestation of the everlasting, personal 'truth' that the filial Godhead is a man's redeemer. This is an interpretation of the Incarnation to be expected from one who grounded his theology in the Fourth Gospel whilst viewing it as a statement of the Christian religion with the minimal of empirical fact. In the *Table Talk* of January 6, 1823, Coleridge preceded the first German, D. F. Strauss, by nearly twelve years in deciding that St John's Gospel is the least concerned with facts.

> The first three Gospels show the history, that is, the fulfilment of the prophecies in the facts. St John declares explicitly the doctrine, oracularly, and without comment, because, being pure reason, it can only be proved by itself. . . . St Paul writes more particularly for the dialectical understanding; and proves those doctrines, which were capable of such proof, by common logic.[30]

So, although Coleridge was quite right in perceiving that a leading aim of St John was to set forth the 'truths' manifest by the Incarnate Lord, he failed to grasp and balance against this the essential message of St Paul with regard to the achievement of Christ in his life, crucifixion and resurrection. 'To St Paul the earthly life of Jesus is primarily an act of divine grace, to St John it is a declaration of divine truth.'[31] What in St John was merely a question of emphasis became in Coleridge a serious theological defect. So eager was he to view revelation in terms of the 'existential now', expressed in the language of a Platonist metaphysic, that he stated the Incarnation as a union of the Logos with 'ideal man' and lost the essential New Testament, and especially Pauline, teaching of the 'once-for-allness' of the Christ event, as an occurrence in space and time.

On a second glance there are reasons that make it easy to

understand why Coleridge generally paid little more than lip-service to the historical Jesus and found the minimal space for the supreme uniqueness of the Christ event, with all that God accomplished through it. As we know, he stands in two theological traditions, one characteristically Continental and the other English. We know that he was influenced to a tremendous degree by Lessing's severance of 'truth' from 'event'. Secondly, through his devotion to the Fourth Gospel, whose teaching he interpreted in the light of a Platonism largely derived from Plotinus and the Greek Fathers *via* the Cambridge Platonists, he became the first of a series of Anglican divines which included Maurice, Westcott and William Temple, whose understanding of the Incarnation had the common basis of the Fourth Gospel, to the comparative neglect of St Paul, dovetailed with Platonism of different varieties. In regarding Jesus as fully human, but primarily a mere 'symbol' of spiritual truth, Coleridge was far from being unique among nineteenth and twentieth century religious thinkers. 'At first sight,' wrote Professor Boys Smith of the period 1820-1930,

> . . . it is curious that the century dominated, above all others, by the historical point of view, . . . should also have been the century which found most difficulty in providing a secure place in its thought for the historical element in Christianity.[32]

But this is another story.

5. Scripture and Reason

In every generation, when the Englishman thinks about religion he is usually drawn to see the Christian Revelation primarily in terms of his understanding of the claims of the Bible. It is so often a secondary consideration to look at the claims of the Church and the norms for interpretation it provides. Coleridge too followed this national characteristic, which to this day gives an ingrained Protestant element to our Anglo-Saxon religion. Even in his final years of fairly close adherence to the faith of the Church of England, he felt no qualms in declaring a right to oppose its almost unanimously held doctrine of the Bible's total verbal inspiration. It is almost a national privilege to put forward an independent interpretation of the Bible. But by 1820 the radical spirit of the Enlightenment had passed on, and the era of historical and literary criticism was decades away as far as England was concerned. Coleridge was alone in his maturity in taking up this privilege. We are in the time of pre-Tractarian High Church and Evangelical conservatism, which shared without a second thought the assumption that all the words in the Bible were dictated *verbatim* to their attributed authors. Christians of all varieties revered Scripture in such a way that it was set apart from all other literature and isolated from any historical or literary analysis. It dismayed Coleridge to discover that this 'Bibliolatry',[1] as he called it, had gained the allegiance of the leading members of every English denomination.

> I have frequently attended meetings of the British and Foreign Bible Society, where I have heard speakers of every denomination, Calvinist and Arminian, Quaker and Methodist, Dissenting Ministers and Clergymen, nay, dignitaries of the Established Church, – and still have I heard the same doctrine, – that the Bible was not to be regarded or reasoned about in the way that other good books are or may be. . . . What is more, their principal arguments were grounded on the position, that the Bible throughout was dictated by Omniscience.[2]

One of the most objectionable points about this view as far as Coleridge was concerned was that it left no room for the individual writer of Scripture bringing his own individual *human* insight and experience to his task. Coleridge extended his belief that, wherever possible, God works through the normal functioning of natural agents, to the inspiration of the Bible by the Holy Spirit. He saw that this idea that Scripture was the passive writing down of a series of divinely dictated messages stemmed from a confusion of dictation and inspiration. With considerable wit he told his companions at table that 'there may be dictation without inspiration, and inspiration without dictation. . . . Balaam and his ass were the passive organs of dictation; but no one, I suppose, will venture to call either of these worthies inspired.'[3]

We may put this in a slightly different way by saying that Coleridge believed that the doctrine of verbal inspiration was a denial of the life, variation and personal viewpoint which each of the writers of Scripture contributed, and in which they embedded the spiritual truths. He realised that, like other good books, the Bible has a profoundly human form and structure, which contributed to it being a living, organic whole, whereas 'the Doctrine in question petrifies at once the whole body of Holy Writ with all its harmonies and systematic gradations . . . the supporting hard and the clothing soft, – the blood *which is the life.*'[4] Here we see plainly the desire of a Romantic to view the essentials of every aspect of life, particularly religion, as a living, organic whole. The traditional Christian view of the Bible, given prominence by the Reformation, which understood it as a monochromatic but separate series of dictated messages, rather than the record of revelation in the light of the experience of divinely inspired men, was anathema to Coleridge. In our next chapter we shall look at his understanding of the Bible which was one of the crowning glories of his work after 1820. But here we shall examine the roots of this new and important teaching on the revelatory significance of Scripture by glancing at Coleridge's early work and the influences that were afoot to rival the classical Protestant doctrine of the Bible.

As is so typical with Coleridge's theology, his ability to get away from 'Bibliolatry' in the face of most of the rest of Christian England was largely due to his early self-exposure to so much of the European cultural tradition. Two of its factors made verbal inspiration impossible for Coleridge. One was the largely radical and atheistic rationalism of eighteenth century England to which he was so attached in the mid 1790's. The other was that he was one of the very few who kept abreast with the literary and historical criticism of Scripture being published in Germany. Naturally the former impinged first upon Coleridge's thinking, and we find its influence in his *Theological Lectures* of 1795. This was the period when Coleridge was reading all the new and daring literature available from Erasmus Darwin to Joseph Priestley. So it should not surprise us to learn that in these lectures he had very much in mind the two parts of the notorious Thomas Paine's *Age of Reason*, which appeared in 1794 and 1795.

Paine seized on two points. There were inconsistencies and difficulties in the Bible, which even Bishop Butler admitted, and secondly, the fact that people were urged to read it primarily for moral instruction rather than any spiritual or theological motive.[5] Paine then railed against the apparent brutalities, inconsistencies and injustices that, on the Christian view, are attributable only to the wise and benevolent God.

> Whence could arise the solitary and strange conceit that the Almighty, who had millions of worlds equally dependent on his perfections, should quit the universe and come to die in our world because they say one man and one woman had eaten an apple?[6]

Paine regarded the Old Testament as 'a history of wickedness that has served to corrupt and brutalize mankind', and as far as concerned the New Testament he decided that nowhere had he found 'so many and such glaring absurdities, contradictions and falsehoods as are in these books'. Early in 1796 Richard Watson, Bishop of Llandaff, answered Paine's rationalist attack with a rationalist defence in *An Apology for the Bible.* Twenty years previously Watson had ably answered Gibbon's *Decline and Fall of the Roman Empire* with its famous thesis that religion induces barbarism and the decay of civilisation. Along with Archdeacon Paley he was admired for his ability to contend with the rationalist radicals in their own terms. His was a quite distinct approach from the sacrosanct view of Scripture of the vast majority of English churchmen. Coleridge was the equivalent of 'a modern churchman' in the mid 1790's, and, before his knowledge of Berkeley showed him its deficient concept of God and a study of Kant its metaphysical objections, he admired Watson's work. March 1796 saw Coleridge writing to a friend that 'the Bishop of Llandaff has answered Payne – I mean to arrange all Payne's Arguments in one Column, and Watson's Answers in another – it will do good'.[7]

Coleridge was very modest about his own achievement. For in his Bristol lectures he anticipated Watson by several months in publicly joining battle with Paine. This is the last year that we can be wholly certain of his total adherence to the classical English Enlightenment tradition, which, from John Locke through Hartley, Priestley, and finally Paley and Watson, sought to establish the Christian religion on a rationalist analysis of history and creation. At this time David Hartley was the current philosophical hero, and the Bristol lectures refer 'to an admirable work of Archdeacon Paley entitled Horae Paulinae, which may be justly deemed the most decisive piece of reasoning ever yet produced on a subject of Theology'.[8] This last honeymoon was notoriously brief. Yet as Coleridge made his only serious sortie over a battleground of Enlightenment presuppositions he defended with great vigour the theism and deism of the Lockian tradition against their atheistic interpretation by Paine. 'What to the eye of Thomas Paine appears a chaos of Unintelligibles, Sir Isaac Newton and John Locke and David Hartley discover to be miraculous order and more than human.'[9]

For our present purpose the second and third of these theological lectures are of most point in showing how Coleridge went about this task. In the second lecture his essential argument was that the divine origin of the Jewish constitution is amply demonstrated by the benefits it accorded. Naturally he assumed that the Pentateuch is a chronicle of empirical occurrences and moral precepts.

> I trust, the Wisdom and Benevolence of the civil Government of The Jews as established by Moses has been sufficiently proved – and to a man (who) accurately contemplates the power of the human mind in different circumstances this alone would be a miracle sufficient to prove the divinity of his Legation. For the Jews seem to have been grossly ignorant of anything, and disposed to the grossest Idolatry. And though Moses is said to have been learned in all the learning of the Ægyptians, yet the Ægyptian Government was an absolute Monarchy – and the people never admitted into any share of the Government. So that where Moses in that infant state of the world could have gained the model of so perfect a government I cannot conceive, unless we allow (it) to have come from God.

In the third lecture Coleridge moved his ground to consider New Testament times. He adduced the well known evidence of first and second century secular writers in order to show that early

Christianity constituted a movement of a highly unusual kind. With a typical eighteenth century rationalist understanding of history, he treated each fact as a distinct piece of 'evidence' rather than as a part of a unified and interrelated series of happenings. I hope the reader will bear again with a fairly long quotation in order to appreciate the flavour of these little known lectures.

A sect in its external circumstances helpless and branded with infancy, in its internal character deserving this infancy for its mischievous and atrocious principles – and yet the sect multiplied with a rapidity to which I can find no parallel.

However I doubt not that when in addition to public ignomony such hidden punishments were added, a Religion so absurd in its Superstitions, so contradictory to truth and good morals in its precepts must have been finally stopped. – Suppose that shortly after this . . . to commence the perusal of Pliny the younger . . . how should I be astonished to find the direct opposite to be the real fact! 70 years after the Death of the founder of the Religion . . . Pliny informs us that in the provinces of Bithynia and Pontus . . . the contagion of the Superstition had wandered thro' not cities only, but the villages and scattered cottages.

Coleridge proceeded to build up the list of evidence – the Resurrection, Jesus's foretelling of events, the miracles, the quality of Christian precepts, and above all the accuracy of the Scriptures in setting these forth.

Indeed such is the influence of their authority in determining the divinity of the Christian Religion, that we wonder the adversaries of Christianity have not constantly made their fresh attacks on this Quarter. The Gospels mention time, place, circumstance, names with the most minute accuracy – the actions, which they relate are asserted to have been performed publicly, and many of them in the presence of their Enemies.

The case is added to by reference to the courage of Paul, the integrity of Luke, and a host of further details. Yet never again was Coleridge to approach the Bible in this way. Never again was Coleridge to have much in common with leading English churchmen as he had with Paley and Watson at this time. As he grew in the spirit of Romanticism the whole Lockian tradition became abhorrent to him. As inward faith and feeling became the essence of the Christian Religion for him, Scripture could not compel belief but only illuminate it. *Sola fide* of Luther rendered the evidence writing of Paley an anachronism. Yet even Paley and Watson were really only two flickering candles among the mass of English churchmen. Their hearts were with verbal inspiration and the total inerrancy of Scripture. After Paley they passed the four decades from 1800 in even more firmly gratifying this heart's desire. So Coleridge and his contemporaries were on divergent paths.

As time progressed Coleridge became more and more aware of the German methods of literary and linguistic criticism of Scripture. Here he was not quite alone among Englishmen as we shall see. But when he returned to the fold of orthodoxy in his mature years, it rendered 'Bibliolatry' an impossible doctrine. Yet he could not swallow so much of the German work undigested because, as with that of Michaelis and Lessing, it was done in the spirit of Enlightenment polemic. It was a dilemma. As a man of the intellect he was not at home with this Christian ignorance and irrationality. As a deeply religious man following in the footsteps of Luther, Fox, Pascal and others, he could not accept the rationalists' shallow understanding of theology. It was a dilemma he resolved by absorbing the knowledge made available by the Germans, and then using this research into Scripture in his own highly personal interpretation.

We now turn to examine how Coleridge gained this knowledge and see how a few other Englishmen of the time came to appreciate it. Of these rare figures, Herbert Marsh, who eventually became Bishop of Peterborough, was perhaps the most interesting. He studied at Gottingen under J. D. Michaelis, who opposed the traditional orthodoxy in believing that there is no need to ascribe the contradiction in the Gospels to the reader's ignorance. Even if Mark, Luke and Acts are not supernaturally attested free from error, 'we can still learn just as much from them as we can from any other historical work regarding the general historical reliability of which we have become convinced on purely rational grounds.'

On his return to England, Marsh made known these views by translating Michaelis's *Introduction to the New Testament* (4 vols., 1793-1801),[10] and the first of these volumes Coleridge borrowed from the Bristol Library in the year of publication.[11] Another of the same vein was Alexander Geddes, a Roman Catholic priest from Aberdeenshire, who made a new translation of the Bible, to which he intended to attach critical and explanatory notes. The first volume of the work appeared in 1792, and others soon followed. The ensuing outcry resulted in his removal from office, and the work was incomplete at his death in 1802. The

Roman Catholic Church defended 'Bibliolatry' with dismissal; the English Church merely gave the more influential Marsh a decade of derision and being regarded as suspect. But the same sentiment over Scripture prevailed in every religious group and class in the country.

The position of things in England is well illustrated by a glance at William van Mildert, who was one of the most influential divines in the early part of the last century. To educated churchmen of the time the ideas of the French Revolution had engendered a fear of atheism. Few of them had more than a superficial knowledge of German theology. But the two were looked upon as allies, lying low, but waiting to sweep Englishmen into radicalism and disbelief. Van Mildert knew of the new ideas. From his Bampton Lectures we gather that something has made him modify the traditional premises of the doctrine of verbal inspiration. He tentatively agreed that the Bible should not be treated in a manner contrary to that of other literature. This was certainly a concession, but, retreating behind old defences, he emphasised that, if the Bible has a character all of its own, this must provide the basis for its interpretation.

> . . . it be most true, that the theologian would be justly exposed to contempt, who, in his endeavour to expound the Sacred Work, should violate any established canon of ordinary criticism; yet if the Scriptures themselves have a peculiar and extraordinary character impressed upon them, which takes them out of the class of ordinary writings, that character, whatever it be, ought unquestionably to form the basis of his judgment respecting the matters which they contain.[12]

Van Mildert's discretion allowed his eventual elevation to be the last Bishop of Durham with palatine rank: Marsh had to rest content with the lesser see of Peterborough. It is obvious which ideas dominated the minds of churchmen at the time.

However Coleridge was outside of all this. He examined as many ideas he could gain knowledge of, regardless of their antecedents. If the reader has a taste for labels we can say that Coleridge was concerned with being a Christian European rather than a clerically-minded Englishman. He went on quietly building up his knowledge of the new ways of approaching theology, and was the first from this country to appreciate Schleiermacher's great classic *The Christian Faith*. In the 1820's other began to visit German theological schools. Pusey and Hugh James Rose published accounts of their work, and Thirlwall translated Schleiermacher's *Introduction to St Luke*. The more perceptive English divines began to be uncomfortable. Would there be a tremendous national crisis of faith? Ideas took much longer in those days to reach the ordinary man. For some the episode of the Tractarian movement would remove them from asking questions about the Bible. Their crisis was in coming to terms with the meaning of the Church. But for its future health the English Church needed an interpretation of Scripture which was accommodating of the new work on historical and literary criticism, and at the same time preserved a view of its inspiration that allowed it to live in men's hearts and illuminate their spiritual and moral being. This is precisely what Coleridge provided. It is a testimony to his greatness. While Oxford men had their eyes on Newman, in a much quieter manner some of the most able from her sister university found their spiritual guide in Coleridge. This influence was to diffuse and hold churchmen in good stead in the crises of belief which beset later Victorian England. The work of Coleridge in his maturity in approaching the Bible should alone ensure his greatness. Examining this is the work of our last chapter.

6. Scripture and Inspiration

We must preface our account by saying that Coleridge always held Scripture in profound respect. He saw it as a unique collection of literature with a greater value than that of the world's other great religious writings. 'It is highly worthy of observation,' said *The Friend*,

> that the inspired writings received by Christians are distinguishable from all other books pretending to inspiration, from the Scriptures of the Brahmins, and even from the Koran, in their strong and frequent recommendations of truth.[1]

It is important to remind ourselves that for Coleridge a 'truth' in this sense means not a fact *in se*, but rather something of personal significance. In *The Friend* of 1809 we have the seed of Coleridge's great theory of inspiration which was formulated fifteen years later and not published until six years after his death. The posthumous *Confessions of an Inquiring Spirit* has as its key-note, the conviction that 'in the Bible there is more that *finds* me than I have experienced in all other books put together'.[2] We notice that, although enormous, the difference Coleridge discovered between Scripture and other literature was one of degree and not of kind. This flies right in the face of the dominant theory of verbal inspiration, and appears to have been mediated for Coleridge's development through his old friend Spinoza.

> A . . . theory was suggested by Maimonides, which was revived by Spinoza . . . : this theory is that the book does not, even in its religious element, differ in kind from other books, but only in degree. . . . Coleridge would by many be considered to give expression to this theory in his *Confessions of an Inquiring Spirit*.[3]

We never know when we shall discover the shadow of Spinoza behind Coleridge's thinking, and it is similarly true with Lessing.

He took the second of his premises of inspiration from the latter's well-known severance between revelation and event. Coleridge showed remarkable consistency with the rest of his theology in reckoning that inspiration occurs within a man in the here and now. The written word of Scripture fits or 'finds me' in this experience, fills it out, and gives it shape and a meaning that can be communicated.

However there is an inconsistency in Coleridge's understanding of the Bible. His interest in higher criticism could not easily be wedded to a view of inspiration which allowed Scripture to be evaluated by a subjective process in the mind. If the Bible is to function merely as a reflection of feeling there is no point in making an advanced and liguistic study of it as representing the Hebrew-Christian religious tradition. We see the problem in Coleridge's mind from a notebook entry of 1824 where he condemns the Platonist approach to the Gospels, which was so often to be his own standby.

> Wade and myself are agreed to the following:
> 1. That we are opposed *equally* to all attempts to explain anything *into* Scripture, and to all attempts to explain anything *out* of Scripture (i.e. to explain away positive assertions of Scripture under the pretence that the literal sense is not agreeable to *reason*). . . . Thus a Platonist would believe as ideally true certain doctrines independent of Scripture and therefore anticipate their Scriptural realization which an Epicurean will not receive in the most positive declarations of the divine Word.[4]

Coleridge was quite prepared to talk about the Bible as giving witness to historical events accomplished under the guidance of God. But his greater problem was to decide the revelatory significance of the Scriptures as we hold them, read and meditate upon them. The final answer he gave to this was analogous to the one he used to relate the historical figure of Jesus Christ with the personal disclosure through the Word in the here and now. The people and events related in the Bible are 'symbols'[5] of Christ, which can have little meaning for us unless the written page of Scripture becomes inspired to the reader through the activity of the Holy Spirit. The Biblical narratives are, as it were, potential, and for their actuation in inspiration require the present activity of the Holy Spirit. Thus Coleridge complained that the Reformed tradition has always asserted 'that the Scriptures were written under the special impulse of the Holy Ghost' because 'they did not always distinguish the inspiration, the imbreathment, of the predisposing and assisting SPIRIT from the revelation of the informing WORD'.[6]

This phrase 'informing Word' provides the key to understanding Coleridge's view of the revelatory significance of the written letter of Scripture. It is to be viewed alongside his interpretation of the significance of the historical revelation in Jesus Christ. The whole of the Bible, Coleridge wanted to argue, is what we might term an extension of the great 'Symbol', the historical figure of the Incarnate Word. As he is prefigurative, and, in some sense, preconditional to and illuminating with knowledge the personal disclosure through the Word in the here and now, so the written letter of Scripture witnesses to the *information or manifestation of truth* imparted through the Incarnate Word, which can only be made meaningful in a personal and spiritual sense by the present activity of the Holy Spirit. In other words, Coleridge regarded the Bible as the *essential precondition* of the Spirit's disclosure in inspiration. It is *not* primarily a statement of the writers' beliefs concerning what God *has achieved* in history, but rather a *statement and pattern* of what he *can achieve* and impart to the believer in the existential present.

For all this, Coleridge still looked upon the Bible as the necessary source of doctrine to render the activity of the inspiring Spirit meaningful to the believer. In this way he firmly adhered to the Reformers' principle which the Church of England expressed in the sixth of the 'Articles of Religion' that 'Holy Scripture containeth all things necessary to salvation'. If no doctrinal development be allowed, argued Coleridge, quoting the Vincentian Canon,[7] the basis of the Christian Religion would still be guaranteed by the moral and historical evidences provided by the Bible. Although he could never really come to terms with the idea of history bearing the full weight of revelation, he still recognised that Christianity is a historical religion in the sense of being an empirical movement. To this the Bible testifies, besides providing the essential doctrine of the Christian religion.

Christianity has . . . its historical evidences, and aims and objects of a religious dispensation. And to all these Christianity itself, as an existing Power in the world, and Christendom as an existing Fact, with the no less evident fact of a progressive expansion give a force of moral demonstration that almost supersedes particular testimony. These proofs and evidences would remain unshaken, even though the sum of our religion were to be drawn from the theologians of each successive century, on the principle of receiving only as divine, which should be found in all, – *quod*

83

semper, quod ubique, quod ab omnibus. Be only, my Friend! as
orthodox a believer as you would have abundant reason to be,
though from some accident of birth, country, or education the
precious boon of the Bible, with its additional evidence, had up
to this moment been concealed from you; – and then read its
contents with only the same piety which you freely accord on
other occasions to the writings of men, considered the best and
wisest of their several ages! [8]

In the last sentence we find Coleridge including the Bible in his
view that the *best*, though not the only evidence of the validity
of the Christian religion lies in the moral and spiritual benefits it
confers in all circumstances. The thoughts of the early Bristol
lectures are peeping through. The external evidences for Christianity include its activity as a world movement and its bearing of
moral strength. But there is a vast difference between the theological lectures of 1795 and the *Confessions*. In the lectures the
external evidences were of prime importance in evaluating
Christianity: for the *Confessions* they are an appendage. In 1795
Christianity had to hold its own in Coleridge's mind with the debate
of a law-court or the reasoning of a scientist: in his later life it had
to address itself at the bar of a man's heart.

The Bible has a special function in this. The Christian heart
inspired by the Holy Spirit seeks an expression of its experience.
The Bible does this far more successfully than any other book for
it is an account guided, but not dictated by God. The heart and
Scripture reverberate in harmony through the inspiring Spirit. We
can illustrate this by drawing a parallel with Coleridge's work on
criticism in the *Biographia*. As the primary imagination unifies
the mind with the external creation, so the inspiring Spirit unites
the heart with the whole action of God in history as portrayed in
the Bible. Thus Scripture has for Coleridge both a poetic and a
historical function. In his mature years he objected to 'Bibliolatry'
on both counts. To reckon the Biblical writers as merely the passive agents of a dictating Spirit denied any poetic content whatso-
ever. Most particularly Coleridge opposed his English contemporaries, those rationalist 'Grotian' divines, who propped up this
doctrine with sleight of hand to account for contradictions and
awkward passages. This was to put Scripture in a coffin away from
the proper function of literature, which is to express life. 'Whatever the doctrine of infallible dictation may be in itself,' wrote
Coleridge, 'in *their* hands it is to the last degree nugatory, and to
be paralleled only by the Romish tenet of Infallibility'.[9]

As we turn to look more closely at Coleridge's critical and historical approach to Scripture, we notice that the same people come in for criticism. The critical approach that trickled into England in the 1820's made it impossible to identify revelation with the written word. But we have seen that Coleridge's knowledge of the new German movement surpassed that of his contemporaries, and he defended the right of every scholar to use the knowledge at his disposal: 'what the right interpretation is, or whether the very words now extant are corrupt or genuine – must be determined by the industry and understanding of fallible, and alas! more or less prejudiced theologians.'[10] He was sufficiently perceptive to realise that many of those who held that the Bible should be taken as verbally inspired *in toto* did so because they feared for the consequences if it were accorded 'to all alike, simple and learned, the privilege of picking and choosing the Scriptures that are to be received as binding on their consciences'.[11] To these people Coleridge posed the question:

> Is it safer for the Individual, and more conducive to the interests of the Church of Christ, in its two-fold character of pastoral and militant, to conclude thus: — The Bible is the Word of God, and therefore true, holy, and in all parts unquestionable:— or thus, – The Bible, considered in reference to its declared ends and purposes, is true and holy, and for all who seek truth with humble spirits an unquestionable guide, and therefore it is the Word of God?[12]

Colridge took the second view. The value of the Bible lies in its existential significance for the believer. This corresponds to his treatment of the historical Jesus. He Platonized the crucial Scriptural doctrines, thereby rendering tenuous the connection between their revelatory significance and the historical event of the Incarnation. By employing Biblical criticism to show the untenability of the doctrine of verbal inspiration, he gave himself a basis to do this for the whole of Scripture. But as we know, he realised that no scholar could ignore inquiring into the historical origins of the Christian movement, and this provided a second motive for his critical examination of the Bible.

Yet for all his sympathy towards the new German movement, Coleridge compares unfavourably with his great German contemporary Schleiermacher on one important point. He lacked that essential quality of the best critical scholars, namely a patient and painstaking temperament. His interest in viewing everything in a broad sweep combined with an unwillingness to master the Semitic languages meant that his conclusions on critical matters could not be completely relied on. Even his very significant decision on the historical basis of the Fourth Gospel was based on little more than intelligent guesswork. When it is Julius Hare, the most thorough admirer of Coleridge of the next generation, who warns of this, then we must note what he has to say.

> Some of these opinions, to which Coleridge himself has ascribed a good deal of importance, seem to me of little worth; some to be decidedly erroneous. Philological criticism, indeed all matters requiring a laborious and accurate investigation of details, were alien from the bent and habits of his mind; and his exegetical studies, such as they were, took place at a period when he had little better than the meagre Rationalism of Eichorn and Bertholdt to help him.[13]

So many of Coleridge's mistaken theories stemmed from his compulsion to build ideas into systems. When his premises were wrong his conclusions could be very peculiar. An instance of this is his attempt to see the message of Job in terms of his own speculative theology. 'The personality of God, the I AM of the Hebrews, is most vividly impressed on the book, in opposition to pantheism'.[14] It would indeed have surprised the writers of Job to learn this!

However a few errors should always be allowed to a man who is trying to bring about a change of attitude in the minds of his fellow-countrymen. It does not detract from a pioneer that he goes occasionally on a false trail, for some of Coleridge's intelligent guesses were very perceptive. As his editor well knew, he 'was remarkably deficient in the technical words',[15] but could still with some accuracy decide that 'Hebrew, in point of force and purity, seems at its height in Isaiah'[16] and proceed to make a number of sensible deductions. 'I should conjecture that the Proverbs and Ecclesiastes were written, or, perhaps, rather collected, about the time of Nehemiah. The language is Hebrew with Chaldaic endings.'[17]

It would be wrong to mislead the reader into thinking that for Coleridge this historical researching into the Bible is of any more than secondary value. We can see this from a very interesting entry he made in a notebook during the early part of 1824. He decided that 'the Jewish Doctors contended for at least three Grades or Ranks of Inspiration, that of the Law: . . . the prophetic, while the third seems little different from whatever our believing ancestors, especially the Puritans, called special Grace – *Answers* to their Prayers – Suggestions of the Spirit . . . in one word, inspiration exclusively *subjective* & without any external evidence.'[18] Coleridge is speaking of the third with warmth and enthusiasm. To him the vital importance of the Bible is to be a vehicle of the inspiring Spirit that illuminates the heart and mind. He had no desire to be novel for its own sake, and was pleased to find in his starting-point a precedent in both the Jewish rabbis and the English pietistic tradition. Within its historical context Coleridge's theory of inspiration was very important. It provided an alternative to the rationalist and 'mechanical' doctrine of verbal inspiration that was to be of lasting influence.

Yet when even a great mind corrects the errors of the past there is usually some flaw in his work. In Coleridge's case it was a failure to explain *how* the Holy Spirit acts upon the letter of Scripture. Only one of the next generation clearly realized this. This was John Stuart Mill, who in spite of being far more out of sympathy with Coleridge's religious commitment than any other of his close disciples, gives us another example of both his vast critical faculty and understanding of the sage of Highgate. None of the differences between them was allowed to interfere with the spirit of Mill's essay on 'Coleridge', where he quoted from the *Literary Remains* and added a comment of his own.

> O might I live but to utter all my meditations on this most con-cerning point . . . in what sense the Bible may be called the word of God, and how and under what conditions the unity of the Spirit is translucent through the letter, which read as the letter merely, is the word of this and that pious, but fallible and im-perfect, man.'
>   It is well known that he did live to write down these medita-tions; and speculations so important will one day, it is devoutly to be hoped, be given to the world.[19]

Mill was writing in *The Westminster Review* of March 1840, and was anticipating the *Confessions of an Inquiring Spirit* to appear six months later. However, even Coleridge's classical state-ment of Scriptural inspiration only begs the question of *how* the Spirit acts upon the letter. The Bible conveys the doctrine to which the Spirit gives life through the inward experience of the believer, thereby testifying to his redemption by the Word. So concluded Coleridge in the final paragraphs of the *Confessions:*

> . . . as much of the reality, as much of the objective truth, as the Scriptures communicate to the subjective experience of the Believer, so much of the present life, of living and effective

import, do these experiences give to the letter of these Scriptures. In the one *the Spirit itself beareth witness with our spirit*, that we have received the *spirit of adoption*: in the other our spirit bears witness to the power of the Word, that it is indeed the Spirit that proceedeth from God.[20]

In a notebook entry of the same period as the *Confessions* were penned, Coleridge made another stab at the same problem. He wrote that the Bible is 'the Mirror of Faith' reflecting 'the faith in all its growths and phases, age after age'.[21] Yet this too is an inadequate summary of the purpose of Scripture, for a mirror is a lifeless conveyer of an image and adds nothing to it.

The simple fact is that Coleridge's methodology rendered it impossible for him to fulfil Mill's wish. Because of the apparently analogous relationships he saw between the letter of Scripture and the inspiring Spirit on the one hand, and between the events recorded in Scripture and the revealing Word on the other, Coleridge was convinced that the Spirit prepares us for the action of the Word.[22] But *how* the activity of the Word in history is preconditional to his disclosing activity towards the present day believer, Coleridge could never answer except by minimizing the activity of God in history. In 1826 he wrote in his private notebook pleading that some way might be devised of interpreting the particularities of the Hebrew prophets' words and actions in order to make them meaningful to the present day Christian. He would clearly

> . . . welcome any plan of interpreting the more express Messianic prophecies or any Code of the Laws or Canons, by which the Hebrew Prophets generally are to be understood that would justify the transfer of temporal Images & Incidents to Spiritual Ideas & Epochs.[23]

Coleridge's understanding of inspiration raises a similar problem. So eager was he to make inspiration part of the believer's experience rather than identify it with a process of mechanical dictation, as in the theory of verbal inspiration, that he postulated a *double* infusion of the Holy Spirit. The Spirit made possible the inspiration of Scripture, in the sense of making it meaningful to the Christian today, by guiding the writers of the canonical books. But *how* this inspiration of the Biblical writers is preconditional to the present inspiration of the Bible for the believer Coleridge was at a loss to explain. It seems most likely that this shortcoming was at least partly due to the influence of Lessing. In his original introductory essay to the *Confessions* J. H. Green overstates his case in arguing for the independence of Coleridge's ideas and leads us to believe the opposite.[24] Several times we have observed how Lessing's 'wedge', as adopted by Coleridge, left little room for the historical Jesus. Similarly, it seems that this same German thinker did much to lead Coleridge to attribute little intrinsic revelatory significance to the Bible without the present activity of the inspiring Spirit.

However this fault is more than outweighed by Coleridge's positive achievement in interpreting the Bible and its inspiration, which we now turn to examine. We can say right away that in getting rid of the concept of verbal inerrancy, he could begin to think of the Bible as a collection of literature that grew out of the experiences of a nation and could therefore recognize discrepancies and inaccuracies characteristic of human writers. He was opposed to all attempts to explain away these discrepancies of which the differences between the Gospel accounts of the same incident provide the most obvious examples. It was not only the conservative English divines who met with Coleridge's censure on this score: he also inveighed against Herder, who, in his *Letters dealing with the Study of Theology,* argued that we must accept every part of the Gospels as true literally or else none of them. At this point in his copy Coleridge annotated Herder's work with the comment 'Now apply this to Wesley's Journal, or twenty other books of the same kind. . . . What! are there no rules of discrimination?' Following this Coleridge asked whether 'is it natural for a plain man who had seen three miracles at three different times under three different circumstances to confound them into one? . . . Surely far more natural were it for such a man to multiply miracles.'[25] The theory of verbal inspiration demanded a writer of such accuracy as to take him out of the human realm altogether. By way of contrast it was the achievement of Coleridge and his disciples to have a profoundly human approach which characterised them among the majority of their English contemporaries in the first two-thirds of the last century.

Coleridge's second significant contribution to the understanding of the Bible was his interpretation of it in such a way that it enters into the believer's experience, enriching and explaining his religion, and meeting his innermost needs. This is indicative of his great sympathy for the pietistic strain in English religion. 'The hungry have found food, the thirsty a living spring, the feeble a staff, and the victorious warfarer songs of welcome and strains of music.'[26] In contrast to the deism of the 'Grotian divines', Coleridge believed in a personal God who is continuously working in the world through his Word and Spirit. The Christian believer, according to Coleridge, has the certainty of knowing that the Holy Spirit works through the letter of Scripture to answer his own particular needs. With the *Deus absconditus* presupposition, God has revealed himself in Jesus Christ; he has dictated various precepts and narratives to the writers of the Bible; and then he has left men to make what they can of them. Thus Coleridge's concept of a personal and immanent God, as we have seen, sharply distinguished him from his contemporaries. He saw the Bible as an agent whereby God immanent in his Spirit can make himself known to individual men in varying times and circumstances.

This brings us to the third, and theologically the most interesting, achievement in Coleridge's evaluation of the Bible. This was his ability to envisage the revelatory significance of Scripture within a total view of revelation, and is one manifestation of his stature as a systematic thinker. Coleridge's corner-stone lay in the fact that, just as he perceived faith to be the precondition of personal disclosure through the Word, so he regarded the same action of the will as the necessary condition for the Holy Spirit to inspire and render meaningful the letter of Scripture. In contrast with so many of his contemporaries, he realized that disclosure to the individual in inspiration rests not on an identification of a book with revelation but upon faith in the Holy Spirit as part of the personal, Trinitarian Godhead to make meaningful for the believer the written page of the Bible. So, in accordance with the rest of his teachings on revelation, Coleridge has explained the inspiration of Scripture in the light of his prime conviction that all revelation derives from the Trinitarian Godhead acting through the faith of the individual. Only when this has occurred can the experience of the Biblical writers be accorded significance for the believer today.

And to make the Bible, apart from the truths, doctrines, and experiences contained therein, the subject of a special article of faith, I hold an unnecessary and useless abstraction, which in too many instances has the effect of substituting a barren acquiescence in the letter for the lively *faith that cometh by hearing.* . . . Who shall dare dissolve or loosen this holy bond, this divine reciprocality, of Faith and Scripture? Who shall dare enjoin aught else as an object of saving faith, beside the truths that appertain to salvation? The imposers take on themselves a heavy responsibility, however defensible the opinion itself, as an opinion, may be.[27]

No matter how well a piece of work may be done, it is of little consequence if no one chooses to take note of it. However this is not true of Coleridge, for when the *Confessions* appeared in September 1840 it attracted attention over a number of years even from those who were critical of its ideas. Some of these criticisms were very acute. One of particular interest came from Paul de Rémusat and appeared in the Paris journal *Revue des deux mondes* for October 1856. This son of a brilliant historian of English thought protested that the Roman Catholic view of Scripture, obviously less clearly defined than the Protestant doctrine, did not fall within the compass of what Coleridge termed 'Bibliolatry'. But what is much more significant is Rémusat's perception that although Coleridge regarded the Gospels as historical documents with critical problems, he gave such problems little attention, and could not envisage how they might effect matters of faith. If Mill had been a Roman Catholic with a less succinct mind, his 1840 essay on 'Coleridge' would have contained words such as these.

For him the Bible contains revelation, but in the Bible all is not revealed. The interpretation of Scripture sanctioned by the Church is better, more natural and acceptable; by and large one should hold this view without falling into Bibliolatry. Also, doesn't he only attach a very minor significance to the textual problems? They might be insoluble, the variations and contradictions may not be reconcilable, but his faith remains unshaken. It suffices to hold that the Gospel narrative is a story as true as any human story; but no one is obliged to understand and believe all the evangelists say.[28]

From a very different background Westcott provided another opinion of Coleridge's work on the Bible. While he was a young graduate at Cambridge he was much more critical of Coleridge than Hort, his pupil, lifelong friend and colleague in theological work, was at the same stage. In his diary for March 13th, 1848, Westcott recorded his reading of the *Confessions* with the perceptive comment that Coleridge failed to examine some of the real problems and 'believes antecedently too much for an investigator'.[29]

These criticisms must be balanced against others who found in Coleridge's work on Scripture a wholeheartedly commendable achievement. In his Bampton Lectures of 1884 Dean Farrar gave the *Confessions* glowing praise:

To it were due the sermons of Arnold and of Robertson, of Whately and Thirlwall, of Hare and Kingsley. . . . It was in this spirit that . . . Frederick Denison Maurice laboured for years amid obloquy and opposition. . . . It was this spirit which enabled the vivid historic genius of Arthur Penrhyn Stanley to recall before us the stately and heroic figures, the stirring and memorable senses, of Scripture and history.[30]

Although the views of Rémusat and Westcott are harsh in picking out the Achilles' heel of Coleridge's work and that of Farrar is fairer, even this needs a little qualification. Although many of the great figures of the nineteenth century English church owed a great deal to Coleridge's interpretation of the Bible, this was generally a diffusing rather than a direct influence. Coleridge's value for the theological generation that followed him lay in the fact that he undermined the rationalist presuppositions that remained in early Victorian divinity and cleared the ground for the growth of a new outlook on the character of Scripture and its inspiration, which was based on historical and critical method. As we well know, Coleridge himself had little confidence in history as a medium of revelation and scarcely any concept of historical development. On this account F. D. Maurice came to correct him. Maurice provides us with a valuable gauge of the achievement of Coleridge's reinterpretation of the revelatory significance of the Bible for the two reasons that the latter's theological influence is more apparent in him than in any other mid-nineteenth century Coleridgean and also, because of the 'Liberal Anglicans', he had the least feeling for history and thereby shows us the least correction that Coleridge's work required in order that it might accommodate a deeper understanding of historical revelation.

Like Coleridge, Maurice was greatly impressed by the teaching of Fox and the Quakers whilst simultaneously contending that Scripture can be interpreted in accordance with the principles and articles of the Church of England. On the question of determining the nature of Scriptural inspiration, Fox set Maurice's thought towards a subjective view before Coleridge's *Confessions* were published. *The Kingdom of Christ* (1838) began by agreeing with Fox that the 'living Word, dwelling within each man is superior to Scripture'. However, we can discern Coleridge's influence in Maurice's essay on 'Inspiration', which appeared in the *Theological Essays* of 1853. He detested the contemporary 'Evangelical' practice of exhorting the youth to accept the Bible on the strength of various and varying invalid 'evidences' until the time should come when 'God's Spirit illuminated the page and their hearts'.[31] The ensuing discovery of the fallibility of the 'evidences' led to the question being asked as to whether some passage 'is not less tenable than the rest', to which Maurice replied that 'to doubt it is to renounce the word of God, to renounce God himself'. 'This course', wrote Maurice, 'I hold to be inhuman and ungodly, one which infallibly makes the doubter what you accuse him of being'.[32] The alternative Maurice proposed was similar in content to Coleridge's teaching on inspiration. He besought his readers to view the Bible as 'a book which does not stand aloof from human life, but meets it'.[33] It does not stand apart from other books; rather, it illuminates them.[34] Yet like Coleridge, Maurice saw the chief significance of the Bible in its pastoral function; in the help it gives to the Christian in his daily life. Like Coleridge, Maurice saw that, for this illumination of the believer, the Word and the Spirit work through the letter of Scripture with all its imperfections and inconsistencies. In this same essay on 'Inspiration' he wrote of

> ... that Word and that Spirit ... connecting, reconciling those various documents which seemed ... so inconsistent with themselves, explaining the facts of the universe with which they appeared to be at war.[35]

However, both Coleridge and Maurice were deficient in one essential element of a truly modern understanding of the Bible. The elements they lacked were quite different. As we have seen, Coleridge took pains to acquaint himself with the developments in German scholarship and on occasion used its findings, whereas, to use the words of the last Archbishop of Canterbury, Maurice 'had only a perfunctory interest in questions of historical criticism'.[36] On the other hand, Maurice had the immeasurably firmer grasp of what we often refer to as historical revelation, which is God's achievement for man in the events of history, especially in Jesus Christ. It required others, such as Westcott and Hort, to bring together the insights of Coleridge and Maurice respecting the Bible and to build upon the foundation they did so much to establish.

Notes

Chapter 1

1. *Reminiscences of Coleridge and Southey*, 1847, pp. 75-6.
2. *The Spirit of the Age* (1825), p. 64.
3. See Mill on *Bentham and Coleridge*, ed. F. R. Leavis, 1950, p. 39: "to Bentham it was given to discern more particularly those truths with which existing doctrines and institutions were at variance; to Coleridge, the neglected truths which lay *in* them."
4. Ibid., p. 103.

Chapter 2

1. *The Poems of Coleridge*, 1912, pp. 110-111. The editor E. H. Coleridge writes: "See this demonstrated by Hartley, vol. 1, p. 114; vol. 2, p. 239."
2. In the *Grammar of Assent* (1870).
3. In her comment to NB.1 174(6), Miss Coburn says that Coleridge borrowed Berkeley's *Works* from the Bristol library in March 1796.
4. NB.1.556.
5. CL.2.459. "*Imagination* or the *modifying,* and *co-ordinating* Faculty. This the Hebrew poets appear to have possessed beyond all others— and next to them the English. In the Hebrew Poets each thing has a Life of its own, and yet they are all one Life. In God they move and and live, and *have* their Being."
6. *Biographia Literaria* (Everyman) 1956, p. 112.
7. Unpublished notebook No. 24, vol. 7, folio 123.
8. Planning a fifth volume in a letter to Robert Southey of July 1803 of a work entitled "Bibliotheca Britannica, or a History of British Literature, bibliographical, biographical, and critical . . .", he wrote: "In this (fifth volume) under different names – Hooker, Baxter, Biddle, and Fox, – the spirit of the theology of all the other parts of Christianity." (CL.2.507).
9. See e.g., CL.2.521.
10. CL.2.473.
11. See Paul Deschamps, *La Formation de la Pensée de Coleridge (1772- 1804)*, pp. 380-1.
12 See NB.1.1369.
   "Non enim essentia divina Deus solum modo dicitur, sed et modus quo se quodammodo intellectuali et rationali creaturae, prout est capacitas unius cujusque ostendit, Deus saepe a Sancta Creatura vocitatur. Jo. Scot. Enig. *De dives. Nat.* 1.3.—Id, p. 2."
13. NB.1.174(16).
14. See entry on Duns Scotus in O.D.C.C.

15. *Coleridge on the Seventeenth Century,* ed. R. F. Brinkley, Durham, N. Carolina, 1955, p. 146. See Ibid., p. 127 where the editor says: "Coleridge read the seventeenth-century divines intensely when he was attempting to establish a rational basis for the most fundamental articles of faith."
16. Hastings Rashdall once pertinently observed: "Once admit the idea of Will into our conception of God, and there is an end to all danger of a pantheistic identification between God and the world." See "The Ultimate Basis of Theism" in *God and Man,* ed. H.D.A. Major and F. L. Cross, 1930, p. 43.
17. *Blake, Coleridge, Wordsworth, Lamb etc.,* ed. E. J. Morley, 1922, p. 62.
18. CL.3.922.
19. CL.1, p. 177.
20. *Coleridge on the Seventeenth Century,* ed. R. F. Brinkley, 1955, p. 385.
21. See Ibid., p. 119.
22. See Ibid., p. 323.
23. N.B.2.2784. "Father, Son, Holy Ghost the [ir relationship.] The • is I which is the articulated Breath drawn inward, the O is the same sent outward, the ⊖ or Theta expresses the synthesis and coinstantaneous reciprocation of the two Acts. . . ."
24. NB.2.3231.
25. "God is the Truth, and the Supreme Reason. Truth = Idea Idearum, Reason = Principium Principiorum." Unpublished notebook No. 26, vol. 8, folio 247.
26. Unpublished notebook No. 26, vol. 8, folio 126.
27. Unpublished notebook No. 44, vol. 11, folio 38.

Chapter 3

1. Unpublished notebook No. 35, vol. 9, folio 129.
2. *The Poems of Coleridge,* 1912, p. 265.
3. For a good account of the Unitarian influences on Coleridge during his time at Cambridge, see A. Gray and F. Brittain, *Jesus College, Cambridge,* Chapter VIII.
4. See Horton Davies, *Worship and Theology in England, 1690-1850,* p. 78.
5. *The Poems of Coleridge,* 1912, p. 121, footnote 1.
6. *Evil and the God of Love,* 1966, p. 213.
7. Ibid., p. 218.
8. See ibid., p. 225.
9. See *The Journals of Dorothy Wordsworth* (World Classics), 1958, p. 57. Entry for October 4th, 1800.
10. CL.2.528.
11. Humphrey House, *Coleridge,* 1953, p. 13.
12. Ibid., p. 46.
13. NB.1.1622.
14. See Stuart Hampshire, *Spinoza* (Penguin Books), pp. 133f. For Spinoza nothing gives pleasure or pain because of its own inherent character, but because of the association it evokes in the perceiving mind."
15. NB.1.1619.

Notes

16. NB.2.2078.
17. See C. S. Dessain, *John Henry Newman*, 1966, pp. 33-4.
18. See for example NB.1.1369.
19. See *Biographia Literaria* (Everyman), 1956, p. 80.
20. NB.2.2543.
21. NB.2.2744.
22. NB.2.2440.
23. *Aids to Reflection*, 1873, p. 225.
24. *The Christian Faith*, E.T. (1928), p. 291.
25. *Aids to Reflection*, 1873, p. 256.
26. Basil Willey, *The Eighteenth-Century Background* (Penguin), 1962, p. 100.
27. See for example *Metaphysic of Morals* in *Critique of Practical Reason and Other Writings*, trans. T. K. Abbott, 1909, p. 45.
28. Quoted by S. Körner, *Kant* (Penguin), 1955, p. 129, from *Critique of Pure Reason*.
29. See Ibid., p. 149.
30. This is from the lecture on "The Gnostic Heresies Attack on the Church of England", which among the confusion in the transcript, appears to be the fifth.
31. See Paul Deschamps, *La Formation de la Pensée de Coleridge*, Paris 1964, pp. 457ff.
32. CL.2.634.
33. CL.3.660.
34. *The Friend*, 4th edn., 1850, vol. 3, p. 81.
35. J. K. Mozley, *The Doctrine of the Atonement*, 1915, p. 159. See also R. S. Franks, *A History of the Doctrine of the Work of Christ*, vol. II, p. 372, footnote 1: "Edwards sought to defend the Augustinian doctrine of the bondage of the will . . . ,as followed by Luther and Calvin . . . , by resort to a philosophical necessitarianism."
36. *Aids to Reflection*, 1873, pp. 138-9.
37. *Blake, Coleridge, Wordsworth, Lamb, etc.*, ed. E. J. Morley, 1922, p. 88.
38. See *Coleridge on the Seventeenth Century*, ed. R. F. Brinkley, Durham, N. Carolina, 1955, pp. 201-2.
39. See *Table Talk and Omniana*, 1917, pp. 405-7.
40. Quoted by H. D. Traill in *Coleridge*, 1925, p. 177.
41. See for example Unpublished notebook No. 26, vol. 8, folios 28-43.
42. See *Aids to Reflection*, p. 121.
43. Ibid., p. 253.
44. F. J. A. Hort, "Coleridge", in Cambridge Essays, 1856, p. 345.
45. Hare's knowledge of Luther is well treated in Dean Stanley's Introductory Essay to the third edition of *The Victory of Faith*, 1874. Hare's early gleanings of Luther occurred during his youth, which was largely spent in Germany (see p. xciv). Of Hare's maturity, Stanley wrote: "The unparalleled knowledge displayed of the Reformer's writings is not only most valuable as a mine of reference, but is in itself a testimony to the greatness of the man. . . ." (p. cxxx).
46. *Notes, Theological, Political, etc.*, 1853, pp. 20-21.
47. *Coleridge on the Seventeenth Century*, ed. R. F. Brinkley, Durham, N. Carolina, 1955, pp. 328-9.
48. *Metaphysic of Morals*, in *Critique of Practical Reason and Other Works*, trans. T. K. Abbott, 1969, pp. 65-6.

49. Unpublished notebook No. 30, vol. 9, folio 15. Although brief, the only satisfactory treatment to date of Coleridge's doctrine of faith is that given long ago by Hort. See "Coleridge" in *Cambridge Essays*, 1856, p. 324. "He (Coleridge) constantly said that faith was not reason *per se*, but reason in conjunction with the will. . . ."
50. John Hick, *Evil and the God of Love*, 1966, pp. 121-2.
51. See for example, unpublished notebook No. 26, vol. 8, folios 28-43, and No. 30, vol. 9, folios 31-2.
52. *Aids to Reflection*, 1873, pp. 256-7.
53. See Pannenberg, *Jesus God and Man*, 1968, pp. 208ff.
54. "Notes on Luther's Table Talk" in *Notes, Theological, Political, etc.*, 1853, p. 23.
55. Ibid., p. 29.
56. Ibid., p. 16. See also footnote to *Aids*, 1873, p. 279, where Coleridge gives an exegesis of 2 Cor. V. as also setting forth this doctrine.
57. See Horton Davies, *Worship and Theology in England, 1690-1850*, 1961, p. 287.
58. See Guy Kendall, *Charles Kingsley and his Ideas*, p. 126.
59. CL.3.913.
60. See *Aids*, 1873, p. 137.
61. Horton Davies, *Worship and Theology in England*, p. 124.
62. See F. W. Farrar, *Eternal Hope*, 1901, p. 62, footnote: "Jeremy Taylor, who . . . not infrequently uses wavering language, seems to have held the theory of conditional immortality, – at any rate as Coleridge observes *in abditis fidei*."
63. See Ibid., Excursus III, "On the Word", pp. 197ff.
64. Unpublished notebook No. 23, vol. 7, folio 4.
65. *Table Talk and Omniana*, 1917, p. 407. *phenomena tōn noumenōn*. For Coleridge this means the phenomena or events that occur in the highest metaphysical and religious sphere.
66. *Notes, Theological, Political, etc.*, 1853, p. 31.
67. CL.3.734.
68. Quoted by Basil Willey, *The Eighteenth-Century Background* (Penguin) 1962, p. 182.
69. R. S. Franks, *A History of the Doctrine of the Work of Christ*, vol. II, p. 377.
70. Ibid., p. 378.
71. "Coleridge" in *Cambridge Essays*, 1856, p. 338.
72. See *The Christian Faith*, English translation, 1928, p. 270.
73. *Evil and the God of Love*, 1966, p. 227.
74. See Robert Munro, *Schleiermacher*, 1903, p. 20, where Hare, Maurice and Erskine are all listed as being well acquainted with Schleiermacher's theology. In the case of Erskine it seems safer to follow A .R. Vidler, *F. D. Maurice and Company*, 1966, p. 246, who accepts Tulloch's view that he was indebted to neither Schleiermacher nor Coleridge.
75. "I had read Coleridge before I came up." *Life of F. D. Maurice*, 1884, vol. I, p. 176.
76. His first reference to Schleiermacher in a letter occurred in 1848. See *Life of F. D. Maurice*, vol. I, p. 453.
77. See Ibid., vol. I, p. 121.
78. See R. S. Franks, *A History of the Doctrine of the Work of Christ*, vol. II, pp. 382-3.

Notes

79. See *The Kingdom of Christ*, 4th edn., 1891, p. xxvii.
80. See *Theological Essays*, new edn., 1957, p. 101.
    "I have tried to indicate the feelings and demands of a man who has been awakened to know sin in himself. . . . He is in despair, because he is sure that he is at war, not merely with a Sovereign Will, but with a perfectly good will. . . . He thinks he has an Advocate, and that the mind of this Advocate cannot be opposed to the mind of the Lord of all, the Creator of the universe, but must be counterpart of it."
81. *Theological Essays*, p. 47.
82. *The Victory of Faith*, 1874, p. 46.
83. *Coleridge on the Seventeenth Century*, Durham, N. Carolina, 1955, p. 197.
84. *The Life and Letters of F. J. A. Hort*, vol. 2, p. 329.
85. *Life and Letters of Hort*, vol. 1, p. 78.
86. See Ibid., vol. I, pp. 120-1.
87. See Ibid., vol. I, p. 430.
88. See Ibid., vol. II, pp. 157-8.
89. See Lecture III of *The Way the Truth the Life*, 2nd edn., 1891, pp. 135-146.

Chapter 4

1. Unpublished notebook No. 51, vol. 12, folio 68.
2. *The Life of F. D. Maurice*, 1884, vol. I, p. 203.
3. F. M. Barnard, *Herder's Social and Political Thought*, 1965, p. 169.
4. See *Cambridge Essays*, 1856, pp. 318-9.
5. NB.1.377.
6. See for example, D. M. Baillie, *God was in Christ*, 1961, p. 115.
7. CL.2.631.
8. For an indication that Coleridge was reading Luther early in 1799, see NB.1.385, where he quotes from "Luther's Letter on Interpretation"
9. *Biographia Literaria* (Everyman), 1956, p. 79.
10. Alfred Cobban, *Edmund Burke and the Revolt against the Eighteenth Century*, 1929, pp. 178-9.
11. *Biographia*, p. 105.
12. *Table Talk and Omniana*, 1917, p. 187.
13. See Ibid.
14. Ibid., p. 164.
15. Ibid., p. 264.
16. *Church and State*, 1852, p. 38.
17. Ibid., p. 34.
18. See *Lay Sermons*, 1852, pp. 94-5.
19. Unpublished notebook No. 26, vol. 8, folio 57.
20. NB.1.1379.
21. See Spinoza, "A Theologico-Political Treatise" in *Works*, trans. R. H. M. Elwes, 1900, vol. I, pp. 81-2.
22. *Luther's Table Talk*, trans. Wm. Hazlitt, 1848, p. 99.
23. Unpublished notebook No. 47, vol 11, folio 203.
24. Unpublished notebook No. 34, vol. 9, folios 108-9.
25. Unpublished notebook No. 24, vol. 7, folio 105.
26. *Table Talk and Omniana*, 1917, p. 287.
27. Unpublished notebook No. 23, vol. 7, folio 82.

28. *Table Talk and Omniana*, p. 76.
29. Unpublished notebook No. 44, vol. 11, folio 65.
30. *Table Talk and Omniana*, p. 43.
31. Oliver Quick, *Doctrines of the Creed*, 1938, p. 109.
32. *The Modern Churchman* for September 1941, vol. XXXI, p. 257.

Chapter 5

1. See *Confessions of an Inquiring Spirit*, 1956, p. 77.
2. See Ibid., pp. 62-3.
3. *Table Talk and Omniana*, 1917, p. 170.
4. *Confessions*, pp. 51-2.
5. See D. E. Nineham, *The Church's Use of the Bible*, pp. 109 and 119.
6. Quoted by W. Neil in *The Cambridge History of the Bible*, ed. S. L. Greenslade, 1963, pp. 250-251.
7. CL.1.112.
8. The third lecture.
9. Ibid.
10. See Stephen Neill, *The Interpretation of the New Testament, 1861-1961*, 1964, pp. 4-6.
11. See Miss Coburn's comment to NB.1.404.
12. *An Inquiry into the General Principles of Scripture – Interpretation*, 1815, pp. 20-21.

Chapter 6

1. *The Friend* (Bohn edn.), 1865, p. 62.
2. *Confessions*, 1956, p. 43.
3. A. S. Farrar, *A Critical History of Free Thought in reference to the Christian Religion*, 1862, pp. 668-669.
4. Unpublished notebook No. 24, vol. 7, folio 132.
5. In his *Confessions*, pp. 49-50, Coleridge wrote: "Who more convinced than I am . . . that the Law and Prophets speak throughout of Christ? That all the intermediate application and realizations of the words are but types and repetitions – translations, as it were from the language of letters and articulate sounds into the language of events and symbolical persons?"
6. *Confessions*, p. 72.
7. Coleridge was a great upholder of the principles of the seventeenth-century Anglican divines, and therefore it is not unlikely that in *The Development of Christian Doctrine*, which marks his complete dissension from the Anglican position, Newman was thinking of Coleridge, among others, when he quoted the Vincentian Canon as being employed as a bulwark to uphold the traditional Protestant doctrine with regard to the sufficiency of Scripture. See *The Development of Christian Doctrine*, 1960, pp. 8ff.
8. *Confessions*, p. 64.
9. Ibid., p. 61.
10. Ibid., p. 61.

Notes

11. Ibid., p. 67.
12. Ibid., p. 68.
13. Preface to *The Mission of the Comforter*, ed. E. H. Plumptre, 1876, p. xiii.
14. *Table Talk and Omniana*, 1917, p. 104.
15. Ibid., p. 262; footnote.
16. Ibid., p. 59.
17. Ibid., p. 191.
18. Unpublished notebook No. 26, vol. 8, folio 112.
19. *Mill on Bentham and Coleridge*, ed. F. R. Leavis, 1950, pp. 165-6.
20. Confessions, p. 80.
21. Unpublished notebook No. 26, vol. 8, folio 119.
22. See *Confessions*, p. 62.
23. Unpublished notebook No. 26, vol. 8, folio 71.
24. Green, Coleridge's friend, philosophical associate, and literary executor, has sought to acquit him of the charge of plagiarizing from Lessing's teaching on the Bible. However his arguments are unconvincing and only serve to demonstrate the similarity between the two. See Green's "Introduction" to the *Confessions*, ed. H. St. J. Hart, 1956, pp. 17-33.
25. H. Nevinson, *Herder and his Times*, 1884, Appendix I, p. 439.
26. *Confessions*, p. 69.
27. Ibid., p. 66.
28. "Des Controverses Religieuses en Angleterre"; Deuxième partie; "Coleridge-Arnold"; in *Revue de deux mondes* for October 1856, pp. 515-6. Author's translation.
29. *Life and Letters of B. F. Westcott*, ed. Arthur Westcott, 1903, vol. I, p. 54.
30. See F. W. Farrar, *History of Interpretation*, pp. 422-4.
31. *Theological Essays*, new edn., 1957, p. 236.
32. Ibid.
33. Ibid., p. 235.
34. Ibid., p. 234.
35. Ibid., p. 237.
36. A. M. Ramsey, *F. D. Maurice and the Conflicts of Modern Theology*, 1951, p. 83.

INDEX

Index